C000156712

The Cambridge Manuals of Science and
Literature

THE VIKINGS

DAMAGED

The Gokstad ship

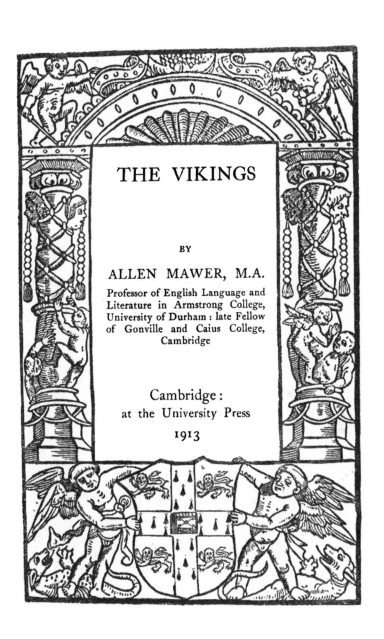

THE VIKINGS

BY

ALLEN MAWER, M.A.

Professor of English Language and
Literature in Armstrong College,
University of Durham : late Fellow
of Gonville and Caius College,
Cambridge

Cambridge :
at the University Press

1913

CAMBRIDGE UNIVERSITY PRESS
Cambridge, New York, Melbourne, Madrid, Cape Town,
Singapore, São Paulo, Delhi, Tokyo, Mexico City

Cambridge University Press
The Edinburgh Building, Cambridge CB2 8RU, UK

Published in the United States of America by Cambridge University Press, New York

www.cambridge.org
Information on this title: www.cambridge.org/9781107606005

© Cambridge University Press 1913

First published 1913
First paperback edition 2011

A catalogue record for this publication is available from the British library

ISBN 978-1-107-60600-5 Paperback

Cambridge University Press has no responsibility for the persistence or
accuracy of URLs for external or third-party internet websites referred to in
this publication, and does not guarantee that any content on such websites is,
or will remain, accurate or appropriate.

*With the exception of the coat of arms
at the foot, the design on the title page is a
reproduction of one used by the earliest known
Cambridge printer, John Siberch, 1521*

CONTENTS

LIST OF ILLUSTRATIONS

The frontispiece is reproduced by kind permission of the photographer, Mr O. Væring, of Christiania; plates II and III are taken from Sophus Müller's *Nordische Altertümskunde.*

INTRODUCTION

THE term 'Viking' is derived from the Old Norse *vík*, a bay, and means 'one who haunts a bay, creek or fjord[1]'. In the 9th and 10th centuries it came to be used more especially of those warriors who left their homes in Scandinavia and made raids on the chief European countries. This is the narrow, and technically the only correct use of the term 'Viking,' but in such expressions as 'Viking civilisation,' 'the Viking age,' 'the Viking movement,' 'Viking influence,' the word has come to have a wider significance and is used as a concise and convenient term for describing the whole of the civilisation, activity and influence of the Scandinavian peoples, at a particular period in their history, and to apply the term 'Viking' in its narrower sense to these movements would be as misleading as to write an account of the age of Elizabeth and label it 'The Buccaneers.'

[1] The word is older than the actual Viking age: it is found in Anglo-Saxon in the form *wicing*. Some writers have said that it means 'people from the district of the *Vik*' in South Norway, so-called from the long fjord-like opening which is found there, but the early Anglo-Saxon use of the term forbids this derivation.

It is in the broader sense, that the term is
employed in the present manual. Plundering and
harrying form but one aspect of Viking activity and
it is mainly a matter of accident that this aspect is
the one that looms largest in our minds. Our knowledge of the Viking movement was, until the last
half-century, drawn almost entirely from the works of
medieval Latin chroniclers, writing in monasteries
and other kindred schools of learning which had only
too often felt the devastating hand of Viking raiders.
They naturally regarded them as little better than
pirates and they never tired of expatiating upon
their cruelty and their violence. It is only during
the last fifty years or so that we have been able to
revise our ideas of Viking civilisation and to form a
juster conception of the part which it played in the
history of Europe.

The change has come about chiefly in two ways.
In the first place the literature of Scandinavia is no
longer a sealed book to us. For our period there
are three chief groups of native authorities : (1) the
prose sagas and the *Historia Danica* of Saxo Grammaticus, (2) the eddaic poems, (3) the skaldic poems.
The prose sagas and Saxo belong to a date considerably
later than the Viking age, but they include much
valuable material referring to that period. The chief
poems of the older Edda date from the Viking period
itself and are invaluable for the information they

give us as to the religion and mythology of the Scandinavian peoples at this time, the heroic stories current amongst them, and their general outlook on life. The skaldic poems are however in some ways the most valuable historical authority for the period. The *skalds* or court-poets were attached to the courts of kings and jarls, shared their adventures, praised their victories, and made songs of lament on their death, and their work is largely contemporary with the events they describe.

Secondly, and yet more important in its results perhaps, archaeological science has, within the last half-century, made rapid advance, and the work of archaeologists on the rich finds brought to light during the last hundred years has given us a vast body of concrete fact, with the aid of which we have been able to reconstruct the material civilisation of the Viking period far more satisfactorily than we could from the scattered and fragmentary notices found in the sagas and elsewhere. The resultant picture calls for description later, but it is well to remember from the outset that it is a very different one from that commonly associated with the term 'Viking.'

With this word of explanation and note of warning we may proceed to our main subject.

CHAPTER I

CAUSES OF THE VIKING MOVEMENT

THE period of Scandinavian history to which the term Viking is applied extends roughly from the middle of the 8th to the end of the 10th or the first half of the 11th century. Its commencement was marked by the raids of Scandinavian freebooters upon the coasts of England, Western Scotland and Ireland and upon Frankish territory. Its climax was reached when in the course of the 9th and 10th centuries Scandinavian rule was established in Ireland, Man and the Western Islands, the northern and midland districts of England, Normandy, and a great part of Russia. Its close was marked by the consolidation of the Scandinavian kingdoms in the late 10th and early 11th centuries under such mighty sovereigns as Olaf Tryggvason and Olaf the Holy in Norway, Olaf Skötkonung in Sweden, and greatest of all, king Knut in Denmark, who for a brief time united the whole of Scandinavia and a great part of the British Isles in one vast confederacy.

The extent and importance of the movement is indicated from the first by the almost simultaneous appearance of trouble in England, on the coast of France, and on the Eider boundary between Denmark and the Frankish empire.

In the reign of Beorhtric, king of Wessex (786–802), three ships of the Northmen coming from Hörðaland (around Hardanger Fjord) landed near Dorchester, in June 793 Lindisfarne was sacked, in March 800 Charlemagne found himself compelled to equip a fleet and establish a stronger coastguard to defend the Frankish coast against the attacks of the Northmen, and from 777 onwards, when the Saxon patriot Widukind took refuge with the Danish king Sigefridus (O.N. Sigröðr), there was almost constant friction along the land-boundary between Denmark and the Frankish empire.

This outburst of hostile activity had been preceded by considerable intercourse of a varied character between Scandinavia and the countries of Western Europe. Early in the 6th century the Danes or, according to another authority, the Götar from Göta-land in south Sweden, invaded Frisia under their king Chocilaicus. Reference is made to this raid in the story of Hygelac, king of the Geatas, in *Beowulf*. Professor Zimmer suggested that the attacks of un-known pirates on the island of Eigg in the Hebrides and on Tory Island off Donegal, described in certain Irish annals of the 7th century, were really the work of Scandinavian raiders. The evidence of Irish legend and saga goes to prove that in the same century Irish anchorites settled in the Shetlands but were later compelled by the arrival of Scandinavian settlers

to move on to the lonely Faroes. Here they were
not to be left in peace, for the Irish geographer
Dicuil, writing in 825, tells us that the Faroes had
then been deserted by the monks for some thirty
years owing to the raids of Northmen pirates.
Dr Jakobsen has shown that the forms of place-
names in the Shetlands point very definitely to a
settlement from Scandinavia in pre-Viking days—
before 700—while the sculptured stones of Gothland
show already at the end of the 7th century clear
evidence of Celtic art influence. Possibly also merchants of Scandinavian origin were already settled in
the Frankish empire and it is certain that there was
considerable trade between Scandinavia and the West.

Most of the intercourse thus demonstrated was
slow in development, peaceful and civilising in character. How came it that in the later years of the
8th century this intercourse was suddenly strengthened
and intensified, while at the same time it underwent
a great change both in methods and character?

The traditional explanation is that given by Dudo
and by William of Jumièges in their histories of the
settlement of Normandy and by Saxo in his account of Danish settlements in Baltic lands in the
10th century, viz. that the population of Scandinavia
had outgrown its means of support and that enforced
emigration was the result. There may be a certain
element of truth in the tradition but when it says

that this excess of population was due to polygamy we have every reason to doubt it. Polygamy does not lead to an over-rapid growth of population as a whole, and it is fairly certain that it was practised only by the ruling classes in Scandinavia. It is quite possible, however, that the large number of sons in the ruling families made it necessary for the younger ones to go forth and gain for themselves fresh territories in new lands.

A clearer light is perhaps thrown on the matter if we examine the political condition of the Scandinavian countries at this time. In Norway we find that the concentration of kingly authority in the hands of Harold Fairhair after the middle of the 9th century led many of the more independent spirits to leave Norway and adopt a Viking life in the West or to settle in new homes in Iceland. So strong was the spirit of independence that when Harold Fairhair received the submission of the Vikings of the West after the battle of Hafrsfjord, many of them rather than endure even a shadowy overlordship abandoned their Viking life and settled down to peaceful independence in Iceland. It is quite possible that earlier attempts at consolidation on the part of previous petty Norwegian kings may have had similar results.

Of the condition of Sweden we know practically nothing but we have sufficient information about the

course of events in Denmark at this time to see that
it probably tended to hasten the development of
the Viking movement. Throughout the first half
of the 9th century there were repeated dynastic
struggles accompanied probably by the exile, vol-
untary or forced, of many members of the rival
factions.

External causes also were certainly not without
influence. From the 6th century down to the middle of
the 8th, the Frisians were the great naval and trading
power of North-West Europe. They had probably
taken some part in the conquest of England and, during
the 7th and 8th centuries, the whole of the coast of
the Netherlands from the Scheldt to the Weser was
in their hands. Their trade was extensive, their
chief city being Duurstede a few miles south-east of
Utrecht. The northward expansion of the Franks
brought them into collision with the Frisians in the
7th century. The struggle was long and fierce but in
the end the Frisians were defeated by Charles Martel
in 734 and finally subjugated by Charlemagne in 785.
The crushing of Frisian naval power and the crippling
of their trade probably played no unimportant part
in facilitating the Scandinavian advance, and it is
curious to note that while there is considerable
archaeological evidence for peaceful intercourse between the west coast of Norway and Frisian lands in
the 8th century, that evidence seems to come to an

end about the year 800, just when Frisian power finally declined. There can be no doubt also that the conquest of the Saxons by Charlemagne at the close of the 8th century, bringing Franks and Danes face to face along the Eider boundary, made the latter uneasy.

There has been much arguing to and fro of the question as to the respective shares taken by Danes and Norwegians in the Viking movement. That of the Swedes can fortunately be determined with a good deal more certainty. The Swedes were for the most part interested only in Eastern Europe and there by way of trade rather than of battle: we learn from runic inscriptions and other sources that some Swedes did visit England and the West, but these visits were due to individual rather than national activity. The question as between Dane and Norwegian has been to some extent made more difficult of settlement through the national prejudices of Scandinavian scholars; e.g. Danes for the most part decide in favour of the Danish origin of Rollo of Normandy, while Norwegians decide in favour of his Norwegian birth. Such differences of opinion are unfortunately only too often possible owing to the scantiness of the material upon which we have to base our conclusions. Medieval chroniclers were for the most part unable or unwilling to distinguish between Danes and Norwegians; they were all alike

'Nordmanni' to them and the term 'Dani' is practically interchangeable with it. The vagueness of their ethnographical knowledge is manifest when we find the Norman Dudo at the beginning of the 11th century tracing back the Dani (or Daci) to an original home in Dacia. The Irish annalists did, however, draw a very definite distinction between Norwegians and Danes—Finn-gaill and Dubh-gaill as they called them, i.e. White and Black Foreigners respectively[1]. They seem never to confuse them, but exactly on what grounds they gave them their distinguishing epithets it is now impossible to determine. They do not correspond to any known ethnographical differences, and the only other reasonable suggestion which has been offered is that the terms are used to describe some difference of armour or equipment as yet unknown to us. The Irish annals also distinguish between Daunites or Danes and Lochlanns or men from Lochlann, i.e. Norway; but again the origin of the term Lochlann as applied to Norway is obscure. The writers of the Anglo-Saxon Chronicle seem to use the term *Norðmenn* very definitely of Norwegians, just as Alfred does in his translation of Orosius, but the term *Dene* came to be used more vaguely and uncertainly. It is only very rarely that the chroniclers

---

[1] The name *Finn-gaill* survives in Fingall, the name of a district to the north of Dublin, while *Dubh-gaill* is the second element in the proper names MacDougall and MacDowell.

vouchsafe us precise information as to the home of
any particular group of Viking raiders. We have
already mentioned the presence of Norwegians from
Hörðaland in England at the very opening of the
movement[1]: once we hear of 'Westfaldingi,' i.e. men
from Vestfold in South Norway, in an account of
attacks on Aquitaine, and in one passage the Vikings
are called 'Scaldingi,' but it is disputed whether this
means Vikings who had been quartering themselves
in the valley of the Scheldt, or is a term applied to
the Danes from the name of their royal family, viz.
the Skjöldungar[2]. Speaking roughly we may however
assert that Ireland, Scotland and the Western Islands
were almost entirely in the hands of Norwegian
settlers (Danish attacks on Ireland failed for the
most part). Northumbria was Norwegian, but East
Anglia and the Five Boroughs were Danish. The
attacks on France and the Netherlands were due
both to Norwegians and Danes, probably with a
preponderance of the latter, while Danes and Swedes
alone settled in Baltic lands.

[1] The name *Hiruath* given by Celtic writers to Norway probably
points also to a tradition that many of the Viking invaders of Ireland
were Hörðar from Norway.

[2] A third explanation has recently been suggested by Dr Björkman,
viz. that it is a Low German word meaning 'shipmen' which came
to be used specially of the Vikings.

CHAPTER II

THE VIKING MOVEMENT DOWN TO THE MIDDLE OF THE 9TH CENTURY

ENGLAND was possibly the scene of the earliest Viking raids, but after the Dorchester raid, the sack of Lindisfarne in 793 (*v. supra*, p. 5), and the devastation of the monastery of St Paul at Jarrow in 794 we hear nothing more of Vikings in England until 835. The fate of Ireland was different. Attacks began almost at the same time as in England and continued without intermission. Vikings sailed round the west coast of Scotland. Skye and then Lambay Island off Dublin were invaded in 795, Glamorganshire was ravaged in the same year and the Isle of Man was attacked in 798. Iona was plundered in 802 and again in 806. In 807 invaders appeared off the coast of Sligo and made their way inland as far as Roscommon, and in 811 Munster was plundered. In 821 the Howth peninsula near Dublin and two small islands in Wexford Haven were ravaged. The Vikings had completely encircled Ireland with their fleets and by the year 834 they had made their way well into the interior of the island so that none were safe from their attacks. They no longer contented themselves with isolated raids: large fleets began to visit Ireland and to anchor in the numerous loughs and

harbours with which the coast abounds. Thence
they made lengthy raids on the surrounding country
and often strengthened their base by building forts
on the shores of the loughs or harbours in which
they had established themselves. It was in this way
that Dublin, Waterford and Limerick first rose to
importance.

Of the leaders of the Vikings at this time there is
only one whose figure stands out at all clearly, and
that is Turges (O.N. Ðorgestr) who first appeared in
832 at the sack of Armagh. He had come to Ireland
with a great and royal fleet and 'assumed the
sovereignty over the foreigners in Erin.' He had
fleets on Lough Neagh, at Louth, and on Lough Ree,
and raided the country as far south as the Meath
district. Turges was not the only invader at this
time: indeed so numerous were the invading hosts
that the chronicles tell us 'after this there came
great sea-cast floods of foreigners into Erin, so that
there was not a point thereof without a fleet.' The
power of Turges culminated in 841, when he drove
the abbot of Armagh into exile, usurped the abbacy,
and exercised the sovereignty of North Ireland. At
the same time his wife Ota (O.N. Auðr) profaned
the monastery of Clonmacnoise and gave audience,
probably as a *völva* or prophetess, upon the high
altar. Three years later Turges was captured by the
Irish and drowned in Lough Owel (co. West Meath).

The early attacks on England and the first invasion
of Ireland were alike due to Norsemen rather than
Danes.   This is evident from their general course,
from the explicit statement of the Anglo-Saxon
chronicle, and from the fact that the first arrival of
Danes in Ireland is definitely recorded in the year
849.   The attack on Dorchester (c. 786–802), lying as
it does near the centre of the south coast of England,
is somewhat strange if it is assigned to the traditional
date, viz. 787, but there is no authority for this, and
if it is placed at any date nearer to 802 (before which
it must have taken place), it is probable that the
attack may be explained as an extension of Viking
raids down St George's Channel and round the S.W.
corner of England.

In 835 the attacks on England were renewed after
an interval of 40 years, but as they now stand in
close connexion with contemporary invasions of
Frankish territory there is every reason to believe
that they were of Danish rather than of Norse origin.
The attacks began in the south and west but they
soon spread to East Anglia and Lindsey.   In 842 the
same army ravaged London, Étaples and Rochester.
In 851 Aethelstan of Kent defeated the Danes at sea
in one of the rare battles fought with them on
their own element, and in the same year they remained
for the winter in Thanet, probably owing to the loss
of their ships.   The size and importance of these

attacks may be gauged from the fact that in this
year a fleet of some 350 Danish ships sailed up
the Thames.   It was probably that same fleet, with
slightly diminished numbers, which in 852 ravaged
Frisia and then sailed round the British Isles, came
to Ireland, and captured Dublin.   In 855 the Danes
wintered for the first time in Sheppey and we reach
the same point in the development of their attacks
on England to which they had already attained in
Ireland.   We pass away from the period of raiding.
The Danes now came prepared to stay for several
years at a time and to carry on their attacks with
unceasing persistency.

The course of events in the Frankish empire ran
on much the same lines as in England and Ireland
during these years except that here trouble arose on
the land boundary between Denmark and the Franks
as well as on the sea-coast.

Alarmed by the conquest of the Saxons the
Danish king Guðröðr collected a fleet at Slesvík and
in 808 he crossed the Eider and attacked the
Abodriti (in Mecklenburg-Schwerin), a Slavonic tribe
in alliance with the Franks.   He also sent a fleet of
some 200 vessels to ravage the coast of Frisia, laid
claim to that district and to Saxony, north of the
Elbe, and threatened to attack Charlemagne in his
own capital.   The emperor was preparing to resist
him when news arrived (810) of the death of Guðröðr

at the hands of one of his followers and the consequent dispersal of the Danish fleet.

Soon after disputes over the succession arose between the family of Guðröðr and that of an earlier king Harold. Ultimately the contest resolved itself into one between the sons of Guðröðr, especially one Horic (O.N. Hárekr) and a certain Harold. It lasted for several years, the sons of Guðröðr for the most part maintaining their hold on Denmark. At one time during the struggle Harold and his brother Ragnfröðr went to Vestfold in Norway, 'the extreme district of their realm, whose chiefs and peoples were refusing to be made subject to them, and gained their submission,' showing clearly that at this time Denmark and Southern Norway were under one rule and rendering probable the identification of Guðröðr with Guðröðr the Yngling who about this time was slain by a retainer in Stifla Sound on the south coast of Norway. This king ruled over Vestfold, half Vingulmörk and perhaps Agðir. Both parties were anxious to secure the support of the emperor Lewis and in the end Harold gained his help by accepting baptism at Mainz in 826. He promised to promote the cause of Christianity in Denmark, while Lewis in return granted him the district of Riustringen in Frisia as a place of retreat in case of necessity. The Danes thereby gained their first foothold within the empire.

Sufficient has been said of the relation between Denmark and the empire on its land boundary : we must now say something of the attacks made by sea.

The first were made in 799 on the coast of Aquitaine and they were probably due to raiders from Ireland who followed a well-known trade route from South Ireland to the ports of Southern France. In 800 Charlemagne inspected the coast from the Somme to the Seine and gave orders for the equipment of a fleet and the strengthening of the coastguard against Northmen pirates. When Guðröðr's fleet plundered the islands off the Frisian coast in 810, Charlemagne gave orders for his fleet to be strengthened once more, but the results were meagre in the extreme. The passage of the Channel was no longer safe, and year after year, from some time before 819, Vikings harried the island of Noirmoutier at the mouth of the Loire, commanding the port of Nantes and the extensive salt-trade of the district. The Island of Rhé opposite La Rochelle, was raided in similar fashion.

The Frankish empire was free from attack between the years 814 and 833. During the same time the English coast was also unvisited, and it is probable that the struggles for the succession in Denmark had for the time being reduced that kingdom to inactivity. About the year 830 the Danish king Hárekr seems to have established himself

firmly on the throne, while on the other hand the
emperor Lewis was troubled by the ambition of his
sons Lewis, Pippin and Lothair. It is probably no
chance coincidence that these events synchronised
with the renewal of Viking attacks on Frisia.
Throughout their history the Vikings showed themselves well informed of the changing political conditions of the countries which they visited and ready
to make the utmost use of the opportunities which
these might give for successful invasion.

Frisia was the main point of attack during the
next few years. Four times was the rich trading
town of Duurstede ravaged ; fleets sailed up the
Veldt, the Maas, and the Scheldt ; Antwerp was
burned and the Island of Walcheren plundered, so
that by the year 840 the greater part of Frisia south
of the Vlie, was in Danish hands and so it remained
till the end of the century. The Danish king Hárekr
repeatedly denied all complicity in these raids and
even promised to punish the raiders, but it is impossible to tell how far his denials were genuine.
Equally difficult is it to say how far Harold in his
Frisian home was responsible for these attacks.
The annalists charge him with complicity, but Lewis
seems to have thought it best to bind him by fresh
gifts and (probably about 839) granted the district
around Duurstede itself to him and his brother Roric
(O.N. Hrœrekr) on condition that they helped to

ward off Viking attacks. All the efforts of the emperor to equip a fleet or to defend the coast were to no purpose, and there was even a suspicion that the Frisian populace were in sympathy with the Vikings. So great was the terror of attack that when in 839 a Byzantine mission, including some Rhôs or Swedes from Russia, visited the emperor at Ingelheim, the Swedes were for a time detained under suspicion, as spies.

On the death of Lewis the Pious in 840 things went from bad to worse. The division of the empire in 843 gave the coast from the Eider to the Weser to Lewis, from the Weser to the Scheldt to Lothair, and the rest to Charles, removing all possibility of a united and organised defence, and soon these princes entered on the fatal policy of calling in the Vikings to assist them in their quarrels. Thus Lothair in 841 endeavoured to bind Harold to his cause by a grant of the Island of Walcheren and Harold is found in the following year with Lothair's army on the Moselle.

The Viking expeditions to England and France stand now in close connexion. In 841 the valley of the Seine was ravaged as far as Rouen, in 842 Étaples in Picardy was destroyed by a fleet from England, while in 843 Nantes fell a prey to their attacks. From their permanent quarters at Noirmoutier the Vikings sailed up the Garonne and penetrated inland as far as Toulouse. In 844 we hear from

Arab historians of their vessels swarming on the
coasts of Spain like 'dark red sea-birds,' but while
they effected landings at Lisbon and Cadiz and at
Arzilla in Morocco, and captured Seville, with the
exception of its citadel, the Mussulman resistance
was too stout for them to effect much.

As a result of this expedition the Emir of Cordova,
Abd-ar-Rahman II sent an embassy to the king of
the *Madjus* (i.e. the magi or the heathen, one of
the commonest Arab names for the Vikings). The
ambassador found the king living in an island three
days' journey from the mainland, but we are told that
the heathen occupied many other neighbouring isles
and the mainland also. He was courteously received
by the king and became an especial favourite with
the queen Noud (? O.N. Auðr). His companions were
alarmed at the intimacy and as a result the ambassador paid less frequent visits to court. The queen
asked him why, and when he told her the reason she
said that, owing to perfect freedom of divorce, there
was no jealousy among the Madjus. The details of
the story are too vague to admit of certainty, but it
would seem as if the embassy had visited the court
of the great Turges and his equally remarkable wife
Auðr in Ireland, or perhaps that of Olaf the White
and his wife Auðr (*v. infra*, p. 66).

In 845 Hárekr of Denmark sailed up the Elbe
and destroyed Hamburg, while in the same year the

dreaded Ragnarr Loðbrók, most famous of all Vikings, sailed up the Seine as far as Paris. While on its retreat from Paris, after the usual devastation, a strange and deadly disease, possibly some form of dysentery due to scantiness of food resulting from a hard winter, broke out in the Danish army. Various legends arose in connexion with this event, and it finds a curious echo in the story told by Saxo Grammaticus of an expedition made by Ragnarr among the Biarmians (in Northern Russia) when that people by their prayers called down a plague of dysentery upon the Danes in which large numbers perished. In the end the historical plague was stayed when Hárekr commanded the Vikings on their return to Denmark to refrain from flesh and meat for fourteen days. Whether as a result of the plague or from some other cause Hárekr now showed himself ready to come to terms with Lewis, and for the next eighty years there was complete peace along the Eider boundary. The whole of the coast was still open to attack however ; Frisia was hardly ever free from invaders ; Brittany was obliged to buy off Danish attacks in 847, while Noirmoutier continued to form a basis of attack against Southern France in the Gironde district. The Viking invasions in France had attained much the same stage as that to which we have already traced them in England and Ireland.

CHAPTER III

THE VIKINGS IN ENGLAND TO THE DEATH
OF HARTHACNUT

THE great development of Viking activity which took place after 855 was certainly not unconnected with the course of events in Denmark itself. Hárekr was attacked by his two nephews in 850 and compelled to share the kingdom with them. In 854 large bands of Vikings returned to their fatherland after twenty years' ravaging in Frankish territory. Trouble now arose between Hárekr and his nephew Godurm (O.N. Guðormr), one of the returned leaders. Civil war broke out and ultimately, after a great fight, the kingship fell to a younger Hárekr, a relative of the late king. A severe dynastic struggle of this kind must have been accompanied by much unsettlement and perhaps by an actual proscription. It would certainly seem that there was some definite connexion between these events and the coincident appearance of the sons of Ragnarr Loðbrók as leaders of a more extended Viking movement both in England and in France. Three of his sons—Halfdanr, Ubbi and Ívarr—took part in the first wintering in Sheppey in 855, while in the same year another son Björn Ironside appeared on the Seine.

The figure of Ragnarr Loðbrók himself belongs to an earlier generation, and great as was his after-fame we unfortunately know very little of his actual career. He would seem to have been of Norwegian birth, closely connected with the south of Norway and the house of Guðröðr, but like that prince having extensive interests in Denmark. He probably visited Ireland in 831, for we read in Saxo of an expedition made by Ragnarr to Ireland when he slew king Melbricus and ravaged Dublin, an event which is pretty certainly to be identified with an attack made on the Conaille district (co. Louth) by foreigners in 831 when the king Maelbrighde was taken prisoner. He led the disastrous Seine expedition in 845 (*v. supra*, p. 21). The next glimpse of him which we have is probably that found in certain Irish annals where he is represented as exiled from his Norwegian patrimony and living with some of his sons in the Orkneys while others were absent on expeditions to the British Isles, Spain and Africa, and a runic inscription has been found at Maeshowe in the Orkneys confirming the connexion of the sons of Loðbrók and possibly of Loðbrók himself with those islands. The expeditions would be those mentioned above and the yet more famous one made to Spain, Africa and Italy by Björn Ironside in the years 859–62 (*v. infra*, pp. 46–7). Ragnarr Loðbrók's later history is uncertain. According to the Irish annals quoted

above, his sons while on their expedition dreamed
that their father had died in a land not his own
and on their return found it to be true. This agrees
with Scandinavian tradition according to which
Ragnarr met his death at the hands of Aelle, king of
Northumbria, by whom he was thrown into a snake-
pit, while the capture of York by Ívarr the Boneless
in 866–7 (*v. infra*) is represented as part of a great
expedition of vengeance undertaken by the sons of
Ragnarr. This tradition (apart from certain details)
is probably historical, but we have no definite
confirmatory evidence.

With this note on the history of Denmark at this
time and on the career of the most shadowy, if at the
same time the most famous of the Viking leaders,
we may turn once more to the history of events in
England.

For ten years after the wintering in Sheppey,
England was left in a state of comparative peace.
The change came in 866 when a large Danish force
which had been bribed to leave the Seine by Charles
the Bald sailed to England and took up its quarters
in East Anglia. In 867 they crossed the Humber
and captured York, their task being made easier by
the quarrels of Aelle and Osberht as to the kingship
of Northumbria. Next year the rivals patched up
their differences, but failed to recapture York from
the Danes under Ívarr and Ubbi. Setting up a

puppet king Ecgberht in Northumbria north of the
Tyne, the Danes next received the submission of
Mercia and returned to York in 869. In 870 they
marched through Mercia into East Anglia, as far as
Thetford, engaged the forces of Edmund, king of
East Anglia, defeated and slew him, whether in
actual battle or in later martyrdom, as popular
tradition would have it, is uncertain. The death of
St Edmund, king and martyr, soon became an event
of European fame and no Viking leader was more
widely execrated than the cruel Ívarr, who was
deemed responsible.

The turn of Wessex came next. The fortunes of
battle fluctuated but the accounts usually terminate
with the ominous words 'the Danes held possession
of the battle field.' In 871, Alfred commenced his
heroic struggle with the Danes and in the first
year of his reign some nine pitched battles were
fought, beside numerous small engagements. So
keen was the West Saxon resistance that a truce was
made in 871 and the Danes turned their attention to
Mercia once more. London was forced to ransom
itself at a heavy price and a coin of Halfdanr,
probably minted in London at the time, has been
found. After a hurried visit to Northumbria the
here settled down for the winter of 872–3 at Torksey
in the Lindsey district, whence they moved in 873 to
Repton in Derbyshire. They overthrew Burhred of

Mercia and set up a foolish thegn of his as puppet ruler of that realm. In the winter of 874–5 the *here* divided forces: one part went under Halfdanr to the Tyne valley, the other under Guthrum (O.N. Guðormr) to Cambridge.

In 876 Halfdanr divided up the lands of Northumbria among his followers who soon ploughed and cultivated them. At the same time they did not forget their old occupations. Raids were made against the Picts and the Strathclyde Welsh, while Halfdanr soon became involved in the great struggle going on in Ireland at that time between Norsemen and Danes. This ultimately led to his death in 877 (*v. infra*, p. 58).

In the meantime the struggle continued in Wessex. In 875 Alfred captured seven Danish ships. In 876 the southern division of the *here* slipped past the West Saxon *fyrd* and reached Wareham in Dorsetshire, but came to terms with Alfred. Though the peace was sworn with all solemnity on their sacred altar-ring, the mounted portion of the *here* slipped off once more and established themselves in Exeter. Their land forces were supported by a parallel movement of the fleet. At Exeter Alfred made peace with them and the *here* returned to Mercia. There half the land was divided up among the Danes while the southern half was left in the hands of Ceolwulf.

Alfred reached the nadir of his fortunes when the *here* returned to Wessex in the winter of 877–8, drove many of the inhabitants into exile across the sea, and received the submission of the rest with the exception of King Alfred and a few followers who took refuge in the Island of Athelney amid the Somersetshire marshes. Alfred soon gathered round him a force with which he was able to issue from his stronghold and ultimately to inflict a great defeat on the Danes at Edington near Westbury. They now made terms with Alfred by the peace of Wedmore, and agreed to leave Alfred's kingdom while their king Guthrum received Christian baptism. They withdrew first to Cirencester and then to East Anglia. Here they settled, portioning out the land as they had done in Northumbria and Northern Mercia. A peace was drawn up between Alfred and Guthrum of East Anglia defining the boundary between their realms. It was to run along the Thames estuary to the mouth of the Lea (a few miles east of London), then up the Lea to its source near Leighton Buzzard, then due north to Bedford, then eastwards up the Ouse to Watling St. somewhere near Fenny or Stony Stratford. From this point the boundary is left undefined, probably because the kingdoms of Alfred and Guthrum ceased to be conterminous here.

England now had peace for some twelve years. Alfred made good use of the interval in reorganising

his army and strengthening the kingdom generally, so
that when attacks were renewed in 892 he was much
better prepared to meet them. In the autumn of
that year two fleets coming from France arrived in
England : one landed on the Limen (between Hythe
and Romney Marsh), the other under the leadership
of Hæsten (O.N. Hásteinn) at Milton in North Kent.
Alfred's difficulties were increased by the fact that
during the next four years the Danish settlers in
Northumbria and East Anglia played a more or less
actively hostile part, both by land and sea. The Danes
showed all their old mobility and in a series of raids
crossed England more than once—first to Buttington
on the Severn (co. Montgomery), then to Chester,
and on a third occasion to Bridgenorth in Shropshire.
They met with a uniformly stout and well organised
resistance under the leadership of Alfred, his son
Edward the Elder, and his brother-in-law Aethelred
of Mercia, and in the end they had to retire with no
fresh acquisition of territory. For the most part
they distributed themselves among the East Anglian
and Northumbrian Danes, but those who had no
cattle wherewith to stock their land took ship and
sailed back to the Seine. There were no further
attacks from abroad during Alfred's reign, but
piratical raids made by the East Anglian and Northumbrian Danes caused him a good deal of trouble,
and in order to meet them he definitely addressed

himself to the long delayed task of equipping a fleet.
The vessels were carefully designed according to
Alfred's own ideas : they were larger, swifter and
steadier than the Danish vessels and they soon
showed their worth when more than 20 vessels with
their crews were lost by the Danes in one year. It
is interesting to note that these vessels were manned
in part by Frisian sailors, probably because of the
low ebb to which English seamanship had sunk.

When once Edward the Elder's claim to the throne
was firmly established in the battle fought at 'the
Holm,' somewhere in South Cambridgeshire, he commenced, with the active co-operation of his brother-in-
law Aethelred, ealdorman of Mercia, the great work
of strengthening the hold of the English on Southern
Mercia preparatory to an attempt to reconquer the
Danelagh. Chester was rebuilt in 907. In 910 a
fort was built at 'Bremesbyrig,' possibly Bromes-
berrow in Gloucestershire. Aethelred died in the
next year, but his wife Aethelflæd, the 'Lady of the
Mercians,' continued his work, and forts were built
at 'Scergeat,' perhaps Shrewsbury, at Bridgenorth
on the Severn, at Tamworth, and at Stafford in 912.
In 914 Warwick was fortified, while in 915 forts were
built at Chirbury in Shropshire and Runcorn in
Cheshire.

On the death of Aethelred, Edward took London
and Oxford and the parts of Mercia adhering to them

into his own hands. Two forts were built on the
north and south sides of the Lea at Hertford in
911–12, and another at Witham on the Blackwater in
Essex. Edward's work soon bore fruit, for we read
that in the same year a large number of those who
had been under Danish rule now made submission to
the king. The Danes in the Five Boroughs became
restless under the continued advance of the English,
and twice in the year 913 they made raids from
Leicester and Northampton as far as Hook Norton
in Oxfordshire and Leighton Buzzard, while in the
next year Edward, for the first time in his reign, was
troubled by raiders from abroad. Coming from
Brittany they sailed up the Severn, ravaged South
Wales and the Archenfield district of Hereford-
shire, but could do nothing against the garrison of
Gloucester, Hereford and other neighbouring towns,
which seem already to have been fortified. They
were forced to leave the district and so careful
a watch did Edward keep over the coast of Somerset,
Devon and Cornwall that they could make no effective
landing, though they tried twice, at Porlock and at
Watchet. Ultimately they took up their quarters
in the islands of Flatholme and Steepholme in the
Bristol Channel, but lack of food soon drove them
away to Ireland in a starving condition. In the same
year Edward built two forts at Buckingham, one on
each side of the Ouse, and his policy again found

speedy justification when Earl Thurcytel (O.N. Đorkell) and all the chief men who 'obeyed[1]' Bedford, together with many of those who 'obeyed' Northampton submitted to him.

Everything was now ready for the great advance against the Danes. Derby fell in 917, while in the next year Leicester yielded without a struggle. Their fall was accompanied by the submission of the men of Derbyshire and Leicestershire. At the same time the inhabitants of York declared themselves ready to enter the service of Mercia. Edward fortified Bedford in 915, Maldon and Towcester in South Northamptonshire in 916. Again the Danes from Northampton and Leicester tried to break through the steadily narrowing ring of forts and they managed to get as far south as Aylesbury, while others from Huntingdon and East Anglia built a fort at Tempsford in Bedfordshire near the junction of the Ivel and the Ouse. They besieged a fort at 'Wigingamere' (unidentified) but were forced to withdraw. Edward gathered an army from the nearest garrison towns, besieged, captured, and destroyed Tempsford (915). In the autumn he captured Colchester and a Danish

---

[1] This phrase is used repeatedly in the Chronicle in connexion with such towns as Bedford, Cambridge, Derby, Leicester and Northampton, and there can be no question that these groups represent the shires which now take their names from these towns. For purposes of convenience we shall henceforward speak of such groups as 'shires.'

attempt on Maldon failed. Edward now strengthened
Towcester and received the submission of Earl
Thurfrith (O.N. Ðorröðr) and all the Danes in
Northamptonshire as far north as the Welland.
Huntingdon was occupied about the same time and
the ring of forts around East Anglia brought about
the submission of the whole of that district,
Cambridgeshire making a separate compact on its
own account. In 918 Edward built a fort just south
of Stamford and soon received the submission of the
Danes of South Lincolnshire, and in the same year
occupied Nottingham, building a fort and garrisoning
it with a mixed English and Danish force. He was
now ruler of the whole of Mercia owing to the death
of his sister Aethelflæd, and in 919 he fortified
Thelwall in Cheshire, on the Mersey, and rebuilt
the old Roman fort at Manchester. In 920 he built
a second fort at Nottingham and one at Bakewell in
Derbyshire. The reconquest of the Danelagh was
complete and Edward now received the submission
of the Scots, the Strathclyde Welsh, of Regnold (O.N.
Rögnvaldr) of Northumbria, and of English, Danes
and Norsemen alike. The Danish settlers accepted
the sovereignty of the West Saxon king and henceforward formed part of an expanded Wessex which
had consolidated its power over all England south
of a line drawn roughly from the Humber to the
Dee.

The submission of Rögnvaldr, king of North-umbria and the mention of Norsemen need some comment. On the death of Halfdanr in 877 an interregnum of seven years ensued and then, in ac-cordance with instructions given by St Cuthbert in a vision to abbot Eadred of Carlisle, the North-umbrians chose a certain Guthred (O.N. Guðröðr) as their king. He was possibly a nephew of the late king, ruled till 894, and was also known as Cnut (O.N. Knútr). We have coins bearing the in-scription 'Elfred rex' on the obverse and 'Cnut rex' on the reverse, indicating apparently some over-lordship of king Alfred. Together with these we have some coins with 'Cnut rex' on the obverse and 'Siefredus' or (Sievert) on the reverse, and others, minted at 'Ebroice civitas' (i.e. York), with the sole inscription 'Siefredus rex.' This latter king would seem to have been first a subordinate partner and then, on Guðröðr's death, sole ruler of Northumbria. Other coins belonging to about the same period and found in the great Cuerdale hoard near Preston, bear the inscription 'Sitric Comes,' and there is good reason to believe that Siefredus (O.N. Sigröðr) and Sitric (O.N. Sigtryggr) are to be identified with Sichfrith and Sitriucc who just at this time are mentioned in the Irish annals as rival leaders of the Norsemen in Dublin. The identification is important as it shows us that Northumbria was now being

brought into definite connexion with the Norse
kingdom of Dublin and that the Norse element was
asserting itself at the expense of the Danish in
Northern England.

The rule of Sigröðr and Sigtryggr alike had come
to an end by 911 and we know nothing more until
the year 918 when a fresh invasion from Ireland took
place under a certain Rögnvaldr. He gained a
victory at Corbridge-on-Tyne and captured York in
919 or 920. He divided the lands of St Cuthbert
among his followers but died in 921, the year of
his submission to the overlordship of Edward. The
Irish annals speak of him as king of White and Black
foreigners alike, thus emphasising the composite
settlement of Northumbria.

Another leader from Ireland, one Sigtryggr,
succeeded Rögnvaldr as king of Northumbria. He
was on friendly terms with Aethelstan and married
his sister in 925. He died in 926 or 927 and then
Aethelstan took Northumbria under his own control.
Sigtryggr's brother Guðröðr submitted to Aethelstan
but after four days at the court of king Aethelstan
'he returned to piracy as a fish to the sea.' Both
Sigtryggr and Guðröðr left sons bearing the name
Anlaf (O.N. Ólafr) and with them Aethelstan and his
successors had much trouble. Anlaf Sihtricsson lived
in exile in Scotland and gradually organised against
Aethelstan a great confederacy of Scots, Strathclyde

Welsh and Vikings, both Danish and Norwegian, Anlaf Godfreyson brought help from Ireland and the great struggle began. The course of the campaign is uncertain but if the site of its main battle, 'Brunanburh,' is to be identified with Birrenswark Hill in S.E. Dumfriesshire, it would seem that Aethelstan carried the war into the enemy's country. The result of the battle was a complete victory for the forces of Aethelstan and his brother Edmund. Constantine's son, five kings and seven jarls were among the slain. We have in the Anglo-Saxon Chronicle a poem[1] celebrating the victory, and it describes in vivid language the hurried return home of Constantine, lamenting the death of his son, and the headlong flight of Anlaf Godfreyson to Dublin. England had been freed from its greatest danger since the days of king Alfred and his struggle with Guthrum.

Aethelstan had no more trouble with the Norsemen and we have evidence from other sources that at some time during his reign, probably at an earlier date, he exchanged embassies with Harold Fairhair, king of Norway. The latter sent him a present of a ship with golden prow and purple sails and the usual bulwark of shields along the gunwale, while Harold's favourite son Hákon was brought up at

---

[1] See Tennyson's translation.

Aethelstan's court. There he was baptised and
educated and is known in Norse history as Hákon
Aðalsteinsfóstri.

After the death of Aethelstan, Anlaf Sihtricsson,
nicknamed Cuaran (i.e. with the sock or brogue of
leather, so called from his Irish dress) came to
England and captured York. From there he made
an attempt to conquer the Danish district of the
Five Boroughs. He seems to have got a good part
of Mercia into his hands but in the end Edmund
freed the Danes from Norse oppression and took
once more into his hands all Mercia south of a line
from Dore (near Sheffield) to Whitwell (Derbyshire)
and thence to the Humber. Edmund and Anlaf came
to terms, but Anlaf was driven out by the Northumbrians in 943, and in the next year that province fell
into the hands of Edmund. In 947 Eric Blood-axe,
son of Harold Fairhair, was accepted as king by the
Northumbrians. In Scandinavian tradition we learn
how he was expelled from Norway in 934 by the
supporters of Hákon, went on Viking raids in the
west, was appointed ruler of Northumbria by Aethelstan on condition of his defending it against attack,
but was not on good terms with Edmund, who
favoured one Ólaf. Probably Eric retired after
Aethelstan's death and only returned to England in
947. In 948 Edmund forced the Northumbrians to
abandon his cause and about the same time Anlaf

returned from Ireland and ruled till about 950 when
he was replaced by Eric, whose short rule came to
an end in 954. In that year he was expelled by
the Northumbrians and killed at Stainmoor in Westmorland. The attempt to establish a Norse kingdom
of Northumbria had failed and henceforward that
district was directly under the rule of the English
king. English authority was supreme once more even
in those districts which were largely peopled with
Scandinavian settlers.

England had no further trouble with Norse or
Danish invaders until the days of Ethelred the
Unready, but no sooner did that weak and ill-advised
king come to the throne than, with that ready and
intimate knowledge of local conditions which they
always displayed, we find Danes making an attack
on Southampton and Norsemen one on Chester. The
renewed attacks were not however due solely to
the weakness of England, they were also the result
of changed conditions in Scandinavia itself. In
Denmark the reign of Harold Bluetooth was drawing
to a close, and the younger generation, conscious of
a strong and well-organised nation behind them, were
ambitious of new and larger conquests, while at the
same time many of them were in revolt against the
definitely Christian policy of Harold in his old age.
They turned with hope towards his young son Svein,
and found in him a ready and willing leader. In

Norway, Earl Hákon had broken away from the suzerainty of Harold Bluetooth, but the Norwegians could not forget that he owed his throne to a foreign power, and his personal harshness and licentiousness as well as his zealous cult of the old heathen rites were a cause of much discontent. The hopes of the younger generation were fixed on Olaf Tryggvason, a man filled with the spirit of the old Vikings. Captured by pirates from Esthonia when still a child, he was discovered, ransomed, and taken to Novgorod, where he entered the service of the Grand Duke Vladimir. Furnished by him with a ship he went 'viking' in the Baltic and then ten years later we find him prominent among the Norsemen who attacked England in the days of king Ethelred. In 991 a Norse fleet under Olaf visited Ipswich and Maldon. Here they met with a stout resistance headed by the brave Byrhtnoth, earl of Essex, and in the fragmentary lay of the fight at Maldon[1], which has been preserved to us, we see that there was still much of the spirit of the heroic age left in the English nation even in the days of Ethelred II. It was to buy off this attack that a payment of Danegeld to the extent of some ten thousand pounds was made. From Maldon Olaf went to Wales and Anglesey and it was somewhere in the west that

[1] See Freeman's *Old English History for Children* for a translation of this poem.

he received knowledge of the Christian faith from
an anchorite and was baptised. He did not however
renounce his Viking-life, but joined forces with his
great Danish contemporary Svein Forkbeard. Bam-
borough was sacked in 993, and both were present
at the siege of London in 994, when they sailed up
the Thames with 490 ships. The attack was a failure
and Olaf came to terms with Ethelred agreeing to
desist from further attack in return for a payment of
sixteen thousand pounds of Danegeld. Olaf was the
more ready to make this promise as he was now
addressing himself to the task of gaining the sovereignty of Norway itself. Many of the Norsemen
returned with Olaf but the attacks on the coast
continued and the invaders, chiefly Danes now,
ravaged the country in all directions. Treachery
was rife in the English forces and again and again
the ealdormen failed in the hour of need. Danegeld
after Danegeld was paid in the vain hope of buying
off further attacks, and the almost incredible sum of
158,000 pounds of silver (i.e. some half million
sterling) was paid as Danegeld during a period of
little more than 20 years. Once or twice Ethelred
showed signs of energy ; once in 1000 when a fleet
was sent to Chester, which ravaged the Isle of Man
while an army devastated Cumberland, and again in
1004 when a great fleet was made ready but ultimately proved of no use. Ethelred's worst stroke

of policy was the order given in 1002 for the massacre
on St Brice's Day of all Danes settled in England.
His orders were carried out only too faithfully and
among the slain was Svein's sister Gunnhild, the wife
of a Danish jarl in the king's service. Svein's vengeance was relentless, and during the next ten years
the land had no peace until in 1013 Ethelred was
driven from the throne, and Svein himself became
king of England. Svein died in 1014 and his son
Cnut succeeded to his claim. Ethelred was invited
by the *witan* to return, and ultimately Wessex fell
to Cnut, while the district of the Seven Boroughs
(the old five together with York and Chester) and
Northumbria passed into the hands of Ethelred, or
rather of his energetic son Edmund. This division
of the country placing the district once settled by
Danes and Norsemen under an English king while
the heart of England itself was in the possession of
a Scandinavian king shows how completely the settlers
in those districts had come to identify themselves
with English interests as a whole. Mercia was
nominally in Ethelred's power, but its ealdorman,
Eadric Streona, was the most treacherous of all the
English earls. On Ethelred's death in 1016 the *witan*
chose Edmund Ironside as king and a series of battles
took place culminating in that at Ashingdon in Essex
where the English were completely defeated through
the treachery of Eadric. A division of the kingdom

was now made whereby Wessex fell to Edmund, Mercia and Northumbria to Cnut—thus easily was the allegiance of the various districts transferred from one sovereign to another. Edmund only lived a few months and Cnut then became king of all England. For twenty years the land enjoyed peace and prosperity. In 1018 the greater part of the Danish army and fleet returned to Denmark, some forty ships and their crews sufficing Cnut for the defence of his kingdom. During the next four years he received the submission of the king of Scotland and made a memorable pilgrimage to Rome. The most important event of his later years was however his struggle with Olaf the Stout, the great St Olaf of Norway.

Norway was now entirely independent of Danish sovereignty and when Cnut sent an embassy voicing the old claims of the Danish kings he received a proudly independent answer from St Olaf. For the time being Cnut had to be satisfied, but in 1025 he sailed with a fleet to Norway, only to suffer defeat at the Battle of the Helge-aa (i.e. Holy River) in Skaane, at the hands of the united forces of Norway and Sweden. Three years later the attack was renewed. Olaf's strenuous and often cruel advocacy of the cause of Christianity had alienated many of his subjects and the Swedes had deserted their ally. The result was that Olaf fled to Russia and Cnut was declared king of Norway. Two years later the exile returned and fell fighting against his own countrymen. Cnut was now the mightiest of all Scandinavian kings, but on his death in 1035 his empire fell apart; Norway went to his son Svein, Denmark to Harthacnut and England to Harold Harefoot. Harold was succeeded by Harthacnut in 1040, but neither king was of the same stamp as Cnut and they were both overshadowed by the great Godwine, earl of Wessex. When Harthacnut died in 1042 the male line in descent from Cnut was extinct, and though some of the Danes were in favour of choosing Cnut's sister's son Svein, Godwine secured the election of Edward the Confessor. With the accession of Edward Danish rule in England was at an end and, except for the ambitious expedition of Harold Hardrada, foiled at Stamford Bridge in 1066, there was no further serious question of a Scandinavian kingship either in or over England.

The sufferings of England during the second period of invasion (980–1016) were probably quite as severe as in the worst days of Alfred—the well-known *Sermo Lupi ad Anglos*, written by Archbishop Wulfstan of York in 1014, draws a terrible picture of the chaos and anarchy then prevailing—but we must remember that neither these years nor the ensuing five and thirty years of Danish kingship left as deep a mark on England as the earlier wars and the settlements resulting from them. There was no further permanent occupation or division of territory and though some of the earldoms and the great estates passed into the hands of the king's Danish followers, there was no transformation of the whole social life of the people such as had taken place in the old Danelagh districts.

CHAPTER IV

THE VIKINGS IN THE FRANKISH EMPIRE TO THE FOUNDING OF NORMANDY (911)

THE years from 850–865 were perhaps the most unhappy in the whole history of the sufferings of the Frankish empire under Viking attack. The Danes now took up more or less permanent quarters, often strongly fortified, on the Scheldt, the Somme, the Seine, the Loire and the Garonne, while Utrecht, Ghent, Amiens, Paris, Chartres, Tours, Blois, Orléans, Poitiers, Limoges, Bordeaux and many other towns and cities were sacked, often more than once. When Hrœrekr obtained from the young Hárekr of Denmark a concession of certain districts between the Eider and the sea, he gave trouble in that direction and sailed up the Elbe and the Weser alike. His nephew Guðröðr was in occupation of Flanders and the lower valley of the Scheldt.

Besides these Viking leaders, who were active in the Low Countries, we have the names of several others who were busy in France itself. The most famous of these were the sons of Ragnarr Loðbrók. Berno, who first appeared on the Seine in 855, was Björn Ironside, while it is quite possible that the Sidroc who accompanied him was Sigurd Snake-eye, another son of that famous leader. With Björn, at least according to Norman tradition, came Hastingus (O.N. Hásteinn), his foster-father. Hásteinn was destined to a long and active career. We first hear of him in the annals in 866 when he appeared on the Loire, and it was he who was one of the chief leaders in the great Danish invasion of England in 892–4. The sudden appearance of these leaders was undoubtedly due, as suggested in the previous chapter, to the turn of events in Denmark at this time. During the year of the revolution—854—no attacks were made on France at all and then immediately after came a flood of invaders. The Seine was never free from 855–62 and the Loire district was little better off. The troubled and desolate condition of the country may be judged from the numerous royal decrees commending those who had been driven from their land to the protection of those with whom they had taken refuge and exempting them from payment of the usual taxes. Many even deserted their Christian faith and became worshippers of the gods of the

heathen. The difficulties of Charles the Bald were
greatly increased by succession troubles both in
Brittany and Aquitaine. Now one, now another
claimant allied himself with the Northmen, and
Charles himself was often an offender in this respect.
He initiated the disastrous policy of buying off attack
by the payment of large sums of what in England
would have been called Danegeld. In 859 occurred
an incident which throws a curious light on the
condition of the country. The peasants between the
Seine and the Loire rose of their own accord and
attacked the Danes in the Seine valley. It is not
quite clear what followed, but the rising was a failure,
and possibly it was crushed by the Frankish nobles
themselves who feared anything in the nature of
a popular rising made without reference to their own
authority. In any case the incident bears witness to
a lack of proper leadership by the nobles.

After the year 865 the tide of invasion set from
France towards England. These were the years of
Alfred's great struggle, and Danish efforts were
concentrated on the attempt to reduce that monarch
to submission. The Franks themselves had begun
to realise the necessity of more carefully organised
resistance. They began building fortified bridges
across the rivers at certain points in order to stop
the passage of Viking ships, and they also fortified
several of their towns and cities, thus giving perhaps

a hint for the policy later adopted in England by Edward the Elder. Probably the Franks were not above taking lessons from their enemies in the matter of fortification, for the latter had already shown themselves approved masters of the art in such fortified camps as that at Jeufosse on the Seine. In another way also had the Danes showed themselves ready to adapt themselves to new fighting conditions. Not only did they build forts, but we hear of them as mounted, and henceforward horses played an important part in their equipment both in France and England.

During these years the Vikings made one notable expedition far beyond the ordinary range of their activity. Starting from the Seine in 859 under the leadership of Björn and Hásteinn, they sailed round the Iberian Peninsula through the Straits of Gibraltar. They landed in Morocco and carried off prisoners many of the Moors or 'Blue-men' as they called them. Some of these found their way to Ireland and are mentioned in certain Irish annals of the period. After fresh attacks on Spain they sailed to the Balearic Isles, and Roussillon, which they penetrated as far as Arles-sur-Tech. They wintered in the island of Camargue in the Rhone delta and then raided the old Roman cities of Provence and sailed up the Rhone itself as far as Valence. In the spring of the next year they sailed to Italy. They

captured Pisa and Luna (at the mouth of the Magra),
the latter being taken by a clever stratagem.
Hásteinn feigned himself sick unto death and was
baptised by the bishop of Luna during a truce.
Then news came that Hásteinn was dead and the
Vikings asked Christian burial for him.   Permission
was given and a mock funeral procession entered the
city.   It was in reality a band of armed men in
disguise and the city was soon captured.   The real
aim of the Vikings in this campaign was the capture
of Rome with its mighty treasures, but, for some
reason unknown, they made no advance further south.
Scandinavian tradition said it was because they
mistook Luna for Rome and thought their work
already done !   Sailing back through the Straits of
Gibraltar they returned to Brittany in 862.   The
Vikings had now almost encircled Europe with their
attacks, for it was in the year 865 that the Swedish
Rhôs (Russians) laid siege to Constantinople.

When Alfred secured a definite peace with the
Danes in 878, those who were averse to settling
permanently returned to their old roving life.   They
made their way up the Somme and the Scheldt and
their progress was not stopped by a brilliant victory
gained by the young Lewis III in June 881 at
Saucourt, near the Somme, a victory which is
celebrated in the famous *Ludwigslied*.   During the
same years, another Viking host invaded Saxony

winning a decisive victory over Duke Bruno on the
Lüneburg Heath. After their defeat at Saucourt
the main body of the Danes made their way to
Elsloo on the Meuse whence they ravaged the
Meuse, Rhine and Moselle districts plundering
Cologne, Bonn, Coblentz, Aachen, Treves and Metz.
So alarmed was the emperor Charles the Fat that he
entered into negotiations with the Danish king Guðröðr
who was with the forces at Elsloo. He secured
Guðröðr's acceptance of Christianity and the promise
of security from further attack at the price of a large
payment of Danegeld and the concession to Guðröðr
of the province once held by Hrœrekr, with large
additions. The exact extent of the grant is uncertain,
but it included the district of Kinnem (round
Alkmaar and Haarlem) and probably covered the
greater part of Modern Holland from the Vlie to the
Scheldt. Here Guðröðr lived in semi-independence
and might perhaps have established another Normandy within the empire had he not been ruined by
too great ambition. He entirely failed to defend his
province from attacks, indeed he probably gave them
covert support ; he intrigued with Hugo, the bastard
son of Lothair II, against the emperor, married his
sister Gisla, and then asked for additional territories
on the Rhine and the Moselle, on the plea that his
own province included no vine-growing districts.
Guðröðr had now overstepped all reasonable limits :

the emperor entered into negotiations with him but secured his death by treachery when a meeting was arranged near Cleves. With the fall of Guðröðr Danish rule in Frisia came to an end, and though we hear of isolated attacks even during the early years of the 10th century, there was no more serious trouble in that district.

In the autumn of 882, encouraged doubtless by the news of the death of Lewis III, the Danes returned from the Meuse to Flanders and during the next three years ravaged Flanders, Brabant and Picardy, establishing themselves strongly at Louvain. In 885 they abandoned these districts and sailed up the Seine, after a nine years' absence. In November they reached Paris with a fighting force of some 30,000 men and a fleet of 700 vessels. The passage up the river was stopped by fortified bridges and the besiegers were fortunate in having as leaders two men of great ability and courage, first Gauzlin, Abbot of St Germain's, and, later, Count Odo of Paris. The position of Paris was at times desperate. The Danes were exasperated by the stout defence and in their eagerness to plunder further up the river dragged many of their ships some two miles overland past Paris, and so reached the upper waters of the Seine. Later, as the result of peaceful negotiations, they obtained permission to pass the bridges on condition that they only ravaged Burgundy, leaving

the Seine and Marne districts untouched ; thus had
the provinces of the Frankish empire lost all sense of
corporate union. The Danes soon made their way
as far west as Verdun. Here however they were
disastrously defeated by Odo, now king of the West
Franks (June 888), and in the next year they finally
abandoned the siege of Paris making their way to
Brittany.

In Brittany they found another army already
busy. The Bretons had won a great victory in the
autumn of 888 when only 400 out of some 15,000
Danes made their way back to their fleet. The great
here from the Seine now joined forces with the rem-
nants of this army, but proved powerless against Duke
Alan, and some returned to Flanders in 890, while
Hásteinn with the rest sailed to the Somme. The
Danes in Flanders were defeated by Arnulf (afterwards emperor) on the Dyle, near Louvain, in 891,
but it had no great effect for soon after we find them
again as far east as Bonn. A bad harvest in the
summer of 892 brought famine in its train and this
was more effective in ridding the land of invaders.
In the autumn of the year the whole army, horses
and all, crossed in one passage in some 250 ships
from Boulogne to the mouth of the Limen in Kent
and, shortly after, Hásteinn with a fleet of 80 ships
left the Somme and sailed to Milton in North Kent.
The story of the campaigns there has already been

told. For the first time since 840 the Frankish empire was free from invaders. Grievous as were the losses of the Franks, it is well to remember that those of the Danes had been great also. Their fleet had been reduced from 700 to 250 ships, and as the whole army could still go to England in one crossing, that must also have been reduced from thirty to ten or fifteen thousand men.

When the English invasion had failed, those who could not settle in England returned to their French haunts once more. A small force of eight ships and some 200 men sailed up the Seine under one 'Huncdeus' and gradually their numbers were increased by fresh arrivals from abroad. They made their way north to the Meuse, south to the Loire, and east to Burgundy, but their head quarters were on the lower waters of the Seine. In 903 other invaders appeared on the Loire under leaders named Baret (O.N. Bárðr) and Heric (O.N. Eiríkr). The name of Barðr is mentioned more than once in the contemporary history of the Norsemen in Ireland, and as the Norsemen were driven from Dublin in 902 it is probable that these invaders came from there. The expedition was not a success and the Vikings soon sailed away again. Of the history of the settlers on the Seine after 900 we unfortunately know practically nothing. The Norman historian Dudo attempted in the 11th century to give a connected account but his narrative is confused and unreliable. Odo was dead and Charles the Simple was more interested in conquering Lorraine than defending Neustria. The clergy were weary of the ceaseless spoiling of the monasteries and anxious for the conversion of the heathen, while the nobles were, as usual, selfish and careless of the interests of the country at large. The Northmen made no great expeditions between 900 and 910, but maintained a steady hold on the Lower Seine and the districts of Bessin and Cotentin. They could not extend their territories and the Franks could not drive them from the Seine. At length, largely through the intervention of the clergy, a meeting was arranged between Charles and the Viking leader Rollo at St Clair-sur-Epte, before the end of 911. Here the province later known as Normandy (including the counties of Rouen, Lisieux, Evreux and the district between the rivers Bresle and Epte and the sea) was given to Rollo and his followers as a *beneficium*, on condition that he defended the kingdom against attack, and himself accepted Christianity. The Danes now formed a definite part of the Frankish kingdom and occupied a position analogous to that of their countrymen in East Anglia, Northumbria and Mercia in England, except that the latter after a period of freedom had in course of time to pass definitely under English rule.

The story of the foundation of Normandy is

obscure : still more obscure is the origin and history
of the leader of the Northmen at this time. Norse
tradition, as given by Snorri Sturluson, makes Rollo
to be one Hrólfr, son of Rögnvaldr earl of Möre, who
was exiled by Harold Fairhair and led a Viking life
in the west. Norman tradition, as found in Dudo,
made him out the son of a great noble in Denmark,
who was expelled by the king and later went to
England, Frisia and Northern France. Dudo's account
of the founding of Normandy is so full of errors
clearly proven that little reliance can be placed on
his story of the origin of Rollo. The *Heimskringla*
tradition was recorded much later, but is probably
more trustworthy, and it would be no strange thing
to find a man of Norse birth leading a Danish host.
Ragnarr Loðbrók and his sons were Norsemen by
family but they appear for the most part as leaders
of Danes. How Rollo came to be the leader of the
Danes in France and what his previous career had
been must remain an unsolved mystery. His name
is not mentioned apart from the settlement of
Normandy.

The Normans continued to ravage Brittany without any interruption and they were soon granted
the further districts of Bayeux, Seez, Avranches and
Coutances, which made Brittany and Normandy
conterminous.

CHAPTER V

THE VIKINGS IN IRELAND TO THE BATTLE
OF CLONTARF (1014)

IN the history of the Vikings in Ireland we have
seen how the attempt made by Turges to bring all
Ireland under one ruler came to nought by his death
in 845. At first this seems to have thrown the
Norsemen into confusion and we hear of a series of
defeats. Then, in 849, the invasions developed a new
phase. Hitherto while the Irish had been weakened
by much internecine warfare, their enemies had
worked with one mind and heart. Now we read of
'a naval expedition of seven score of the Foreigners
coming to exercise power over the Foreigners who
were before them, so that they disturbed all Ireland
afterwards.' This means that the Danes were now
taking an active part in the invasions of Ireland, and
we soon find them disputing the supremacy with the
earlier Norse settlers. A full and picturesque account
of the struggle is preserved for us in the second of
the *Three Fragments of Irish Annals* copied by
Dugald MacFirbis. Unfortunately the chronology
of these annals is in a highly confused state and it is
often difficult to trace the exact sequence of events.

When the Norsemen first saw the approaching

fleet they were much alarmed. Some said it was
reinforcements from Norway, but others, with keener
insight, said they were Danes who were coming to
harry and plunder. A swift vessel was dispatched
to find out who they were, and when the steersman
called out to them inquiring from what land they
came and whether as friend or foe, the only answer
was a shower of arrows. A fierce battle ensued, in
which the Danes killed thrice their own number and
carried off the women-folk and property of the
Norsemen. In 851 they plundered the Norse settlements at Dublin and Dundalk, but in the next
year the Norsemen attacked them in Carlingford
Lough. At first the Danes were defeated, but then
their leader cunningly exhorted his men to secure
by their prayers and alms the patronage of St
Patrick, who was incensed against the Norsemen
because of the many evil deeds they had wrought in
Erin. The battle was renewed and the Danes were
victorious. After the battle they made rich gifts to
St Patrick for 'the Danes were a people with a kind
of piety : they could for a time refrain from meat
and from women.' After the fight we learn that the
Danes cooked their meat in cauldrons supported on
the bodies of their dead foes. The Danes now helped
Cerbhal, king of Ossory, against the Norsemen who
were harrying Munster, and henceforward we hear
again and again how the various Irish factions made

use of the dissensions among the invaders to further
their own ends.

Matters were further complicated by the fact that
many of the Irish forsook their Christian baptism
and joined the Norsemen in their plundering. These
recreant Irish were known as the Gaill-Gaedhil (i.e.
the foreign Irish), and played an important part in
the wars of the next few years. The Gaill-Gaedhil
were undoubtedly a race of mixed Norse and Gaelic
stock and we must not imagine that they sprung
suddenly into existence at this time. Long before
this the Norsemen and the Gaels must have had
considerable peaceful intercourse with one another
in their various settlements, and in accordance with
well-established Scandinavian custom it would seem
that many of the Irish were brought up as foster-
children in Norse households and must soon have
learned to accept their religion and customs. There
was also extensive intermarriage between Norsemen
and Irish. The annals speak of several such unions,
the most famous being the marriage of Gormflaith,
afterwards wife of Brian Borumha, to Anlaf Sihtricsson, while in the genealogies of the Norse settlers in
Iceland at the end of this century, Gaelic names are
of frequent occurrence. One of the most famous of
the leaders of these 'foreign Irish' was Ketill Finn
(i.e. the White), a Norseman with an Irish nickname.
These foreign Irish fought either by the side of the

foreigners or on their own account and we have an
interesting story telling how, when Vikings from
Ireland made an invasion of Cheshire (c. 912),
Aethelflæd, the lady of the Mercians, sent ambassadors
to those Irish who were fighting on the side of the
invaders, calling upon them to forsake the pagans
and remember the old kindness shown in England to
Irish soldiers and clergy.

The troubles between Norsemen and Danes
were probably responsible for the arrival in Ireland
in 853 of Amhlaeibh, son of the king of Norway,
to receive the submission of the foreigners. This
Amhlaeibh is Olaf the White of Norse tradition. Olaf
is represented as ruling together with his brother
Imhar (O.N. Ívarr). The annals are no very good
authority for the relationship of the Norse leaders
to one another, and it is quite possible that Ívarr is
really Ívarr the Boneless, son to Ragnarr Loðbrók.
Under the strong rule of Olaf and Ívarr Dublin became
the chief centre of Scandinavian rule in Ireland,
and the Danes and Norsemen were to some extent
reconciled to one another. The Irish suffered great
losses but some brave leaders were found to face the
Norsemen. Cennedigh, king of Leix (Queen's County),
came upon a party of them laden with booty ; they
abandoned the spoil and rushed upon Cennedigh
with angry barbarous shouts, blowing their trumpets
and many of them crying *nui, nui* (i.e. probably, in

the old Norse speech, *knúi, knúi,* 'hasten on, hasten on '). Many darts and spears were thrown and at last they took to their heavy powerful swords. All was however of no avail and Cennedigh won a great victory. Less fortunate was Maelciarain, 'champion of the east of Ireland and a hero-plunderer of the foreigners.' He was expelled from his kingdom by the Leinstermen, who envied him in consequence of his many victories over the Norsemen !

The activities of Olaf and Ívarr were not confined to Ireland. In 866 Olaf paid a visit to Scotland, while in 870 both Olaf and Ívarr were present at the siege of Dumbarton. If Ívarr is Ívarr the Boneless, he must then have gone to England and taken part in the martyrdom of St Edmund. In the next year both leaders returned to Dublin with a large number of prisoners—English, Britons and Picts. In 873 Ívarr, 'king of the Norsemen of all Ireland and Britain' died, and about the same time Olaf returned to Norway, possibly to take part in the great fight against Harold Fairhair at Hafrsfjord. The Danes seem to have taken advantage of the removal of Olaf to attempt to throw off the Norse yoke. Fresh fighting took place and the Danes under Albdann, i.e. Halfdanr, king of Northumbria, were defeated on Strangford Lough in 877 with the loss of their leader.

After 877 the *War of the Gaedhil with the Gaill* notes a period of rest for Ireland, lasting some forty

years. This is true to the extent that no large fleets
of fresh invaders seem to have come to Ireland during
this time—the Vikings were too busy elsewhere, both
in England and the Frankish empire—but there were
occasional raids from Dublin, Cork, Limerick, Waterford and other towns into various districts of Ireland,
and the Norsemen were often at variance amongst
themselves. Dissensions in Dublin were particularly
violent and so much did they weaken Norse rule
there that in 902 Dublin fell into the hands of the
Irish. The Vikings were driven abroad, some going
to Scotland and others to England, where they
besieged Chester (*v. supra*, p. 57). In the year 914
all the old troubles were renewed. Rögnvaldr, a
grandson of Ívarr, fresh from a great victory off the
Isle of Man, captured Waterford, and two years later
Sigtryggr, another grandson of Ívarr regained Dublin.
The Irish attempted resistance under the *ardrí* Niall
Glundubh, but he fell with twelve other kings in a
fight at Kilmashogue near Dublin in 919. During
the next fifty years Ireland was a prey to ceaseless
attacks by Norwegians and Danes alike. Towards
the close of the 9th century Limerick had become
a stronghold of the Norsemen in the west, and from
there they made their way up the Shannon into the
heart of the country. Cork was settled in the early
years of the 10th century, chiefly by Danes, and from
there all Munster was open to attack. Waterford

and Wexford, which stood as a rule in close connexion with Dublin, served as centres of attack against Leinster. The Irish made a stout resistance under able leaders and Dublin was 'destroyed' more than once. First among these leaders stands Muirchertach 'of the leather cloaks,' son of Niall Glundubh, a hero who came forward about the year 926. His activities were unceasing. He repeatedly attacked Dublin, took a fleet to the Hebrides where he defeated the Vikings, gaining much spoil, and finally in 941 made a circuit of Ireland, from which he brought back as hostages many provincial kings, including the Norse ruler of Dublin. More famous still in Irish song and story was Cellachan of Cashel. He made war against the Vikings in Munster and for a time had the Norse kingdom of Waterford under his control. Similarly he conquered Limerick, and we find him fighting side by side with Norsemen from both these towns. During these fifty years the Norse kingdom in Dublin stood in close relation with the Scandinavian kingdom of Northumbria. Rögnvaldr, who died in 912, ruled there and so did his brothers Sigtryggr (d. 927) and Guðröðr (or Godfrey) (d. 934). The brothers left sons known respectively as Anlaf Sihtricsson and Anlaf Godfreyson. The latter took part in the great fight at Brunanburh and died in 939. Anlaf Sihtricsson was destined to a longer career. He would seem to have

spent his early years in Scotland where he married
king Constantine's daughter. It is uncertain whether
he fought at Brunanburh, but he came to Northumbria
in 941 and captured York. He was expelled from
Northumbria in 944 or 945 and retired to Dublin,
and the rest of his life was chiefly spent in fighting in
Ireland. He was in close alliance with the Norsemen
in Man and the Western Islands, and was, for some
thirty years, the most powerful Norse ruler in Ireland.
Then came the first great blow to Norse rule in
Ireland. In 980 Maelsechlainn II, the *ardrí*, won
a great victory at Tara over the foreigners of Dublin
and the Islands in which Anlaf's son was slain. The
power of the kingdom of Dublin was effectually
broken. The Norsemen were compelled to liberate
all the hostages in their custody, to pay a fine of
2000 oxen and to remit the tribute which they had
imposed on all Ireland from the Shannon eastwards
to the sea. Anlaf abandoned his authority and
retired on a pilgrimage to Iona, where he died in the
same year an inmate of its monastery.

In the meantime events, fraught with important
consequences for Norse rule in that country, were
gradually developing in a distant quarter of Ireland. In
the province of Munster the Dalcassian line of princes
first comes into prominence about the middle of the
10th century, and the two most famous of these
princes were the brothers Mathgamhain and Brian,

commonly known as Brian Borumha. Together the
brothers conquered Munster in spite of the support
given to the Irish by the Viking settlers, and when
their success aroused Ívarr, the ruler of Limerick,
they attacked him and won a great victory at
Sulcoit near Tipperary (968). Limerick was captured,
Mathgamhain died in 976 and Brian was soon
acknowledged king of all Munster. He next became
master of Leinster, but his rapid advance brought
him into conflict with the *ardrí* and by a compact
made in 998, Maelsechlainn practically surrendered
the southern half of Ireland to Brian. The ruler
of Dublin at this time was Sigtryggr of the Silken
Beard, son of Anlaf and Gormflaith, sister of
Maelmordha, king of Leinster. In 1000 Leinster
with the support of the Norsemen in Dublin revolted,
but Brian defeated them and captured Dublin, giving
his daughter in marriage to Sigtryggr and himself
marrying Gormflaith. In 1002 Maelsechlainn submitted to Brian and the latter became *ardrí*. There
followed twelve years of peace, but Brian's marriage
with Gormflaith was his undoing. Quarrelling with
her husband, she stirred up Maelmordha of Leinster
against him. An alliance was formed between
Maelmordha and Sigtryggr, and Gormflaith dispatched
embassies to all the Viking settlements in the West,
summoning them to the aid of Sigtryggr in a great
fight against Brian. Sigtryggr secured the help

of Earl Sigurd of the Orkneys and North Scotland by promise of the kingship of Dublin. Ships came from all parts of the Viking world, from Northumbria, from Man and the Western Islands, from Scotland and the Orkneys, and even from Iceland. Dublin was fixed as the trysting-place and Palm Sunday 1014 was to be the time of meeting. Brian mustered all the forces of Munster and Connaught and was joined in half-hearted fashion by Maelsechlainn, who was really waiting to see which way the fortunes of war would turn. Brian advanced into the plain of Fingall, north of Dublin, and the two armies faced one another at Clontarf all Passion week. The Norsemen had learned by magic incantations that if the fight took place before Good Friday their chiefs would perish and their forces be routed, while if the fight took place on Good Friday Brian himself would perish but the Irish would win the day. So they waited until the Friday and then made their attack. The fight was long and the slaughter was terrible. Brian and Sigurd were themselves numbered among the slain. In the end the Norsemen were defeated and Maelsechlainn completed their discomfiture when he cut down the fugitives as they tried to cross the bridge leading to Dublin and so reach their ships. No fight was more famous in Irish history and it seems to have appealed with equally strong force to Scandinavian imagination.

Clontarf and Brunanburh are the two great Viking battles which find record in Scandinavian saga, and in the story of Burnt Njal[1] we have a vivid account both of the actual battle and of the events leading up to it. Yet more interesting perhaps is the old lay preserved to us, the *Song of the Valkyries*, who that same day were seen in Caithness riding twelve together to a bower where they set up a loom of which men's heads were the weights, men's entrails the warp and woof, while a sword was the shuttle and the reels were arrows. They wove the web of war and foretold the fate of king Sigtryggr and Earl Sigurd as well as the sharp sorrow which would befall the Irish[2]. The Norse world was full of this and like portents and there can be no question that the Vikings were themselves conscious that the battle of Clontarf marked a very definite epoch in the history of the Vikings in the West and in Ireland more particularly. The Norsemen remained in possession of their cities, Sigtryggr continued as king of Dublin, but gradually the fortunes of the Norse settlers tended to become merged in the history of the nation as a whole and there was no further question of Scandinavian supremacy in Ireland.

[1] English version by Sir G. W. Dasent.

[2] This song was probably composed soon after the events with which it is concerned and was first rendered into English by the poet Gray under the title *The Fatal Sisters*.

CHAPTER VI

THE VIKINGS IN THE ORKNEYS, SCOTLAND, THE WESTERN ISLANDS AND MAN

WHEN the Vikings sailed to England and Ireland in the late 8th and early 9th centuries their most natural path was by the Orkneys and Shetlands and round the Western Islands of Scotland. We have seen how early they formed settlements in the Shetlands, and they soon reached the Orkneys and the Hebrides. From the Orkneys they crossed to the mainland, to Sutherland and Caithness—the very names bear witness to Scandinavian occupation—while Galloway (i.e. the land of the Gaill-Gaedhil, *v. supra*, p. 56) was settled from the Isle of Man. Already in the 9th century the Norse element in the Hebrides was so strong that the Irish called the islands *Innsi-Gall* (i.e. the islands of the foreigners), and their inhabitants were known as Gaill-Gaedhil. The Norsemen called the islands *Suðr-eyjar* (i.e. Southern Islands) in contrast to the Orkneys and Shetlands, which were known as *Norðreyjar*, and the name survives in the composite bishopric of 'Sodor' and Man, which once formed part of the archdiocese of Trondhjem in Norway. The Isle of Man was plundered almost as early as any of the islands of the West (*v. supra*, p. 12), and it

was probably from Man that the Norse settlements
in Cumberland and Westmorland were established.
Olaf the White and Ívarr made more than one
expedition from Ireland to the lowlands of Scotland,
and the former was married to Auðr the daughter of
Ketill Flatnose who had made himself the greatest
chieftain in the Western Islands.   After the battle of
Hafrsfjord, when Harold Fairhair had finally crushed
his rivals in Norway itself, so powerful were the Norse
settlements in the West that he felt his position
would be insecure until he had received their submission.   Accordingly he made a great expedition
to the Shetlands, Orkneys and the west coast
of Scotland, fulfilled this purpose and entrusted the
Northern Islands to Sigurd, brother of Rögnvaldr,
earl of Möre, as his vassal.

The history of the Norse settlements in the
Orkneys is well and fully told in the *Orkneyingasaga*[1].
The first Orkney-earl was the above-named Sigurd.
He entered into an alliance with Thorstein the Red,
son to Olaf the White, and together they conquered
Caithness and Sutherland, as far south as the river
Oikel on the borders of Ross and Cromarty.   Sigurd's
son Einar, known as Turf-Einar because he first
taught the islanders to cut peat for fuel, founded
a long line of earls of the Orkneys.   He had a

---

[1] English translation by Sir G. W. Dasent.

quarrel with Harold Fairhair and when that king
imposed a fine on the islanders for the murder of his
son and the farmers could not pay it, Einar paid it
himself on condition that the peasants surrendered
their *óðal* rights, i.e. their rights of possession in
the lands they cultivated. Turf-Einar's son Sigurd the
Stout was the most famous of all the Orkney-earls,
renowned both as warrior and poet. He conquered
Sutherland, Caithness, Ross, Murray, Argyle, the
Hebrides and Man, securing the support of the men
of Orkney by giving them back their *óðal*. He
married a daughter of Malcolm king of Scotland,
and met his end, as we have already seen, fighting
on the side of the heathen Norsemen in the battle
of Clontarf in 1014. After this the power of the
Orkney-earls declined. The Norse line of earls was
replaced by one of Scottish descent in 1231, but the
islands did not pass definitely to the Scottish crown
until the 15th century[1].

Of the Norse settlements in the Hebrides we
have no such definite or continuous record. Mention
is made in Irish annals of the middle of the
9th century of a king in the Hebrides—one Guðröðr
son of Fergus—whose very name shows him to have
been one of the Gaill-Gaedhil. Ketill Finn (*v. supra,*

[1] They were pledged by Christian I of Denmark and Norway for
the payment of the dowry of his daughter Margaret to James III in
1460 and the pledge was never redeemed.

p. 56) was another such. In the latter half of the
9th century Ketill Flatnose was the chief Norse
leader in the Hebrides until his power was destroyed
by Harold Fairhair. Many of the settlers then
betook themselves to Iceland, the most famous of
them being Auðr the deep-thoughted, widow of
Olaf the White and daughter of Ketill. Norse rule
was all powerful during the 10th and 11th centuries.
There was a line of kings but we find ruling side by
side with them certain officers known as 'lawmen'
(*v. infra*, p. 103), while in the late 10th and for
the greater part of the 11th century, the Hebrides
were under the sovereignty of the Orkney-earls.
Norse rule in the Hebrides did not finally come to
an end until 1266 when Magnus Hákonsson, king
of Norway, renounced all claims to the islands.

The early history of the settlements in Man is
equally obscure. At first the island suffered from
repeated raids, then about the middle of the
9th century it passed under the authority of the
kings of Dublin and remained so until, with the
Hebrides and Western Scotland generally, it was
conquered by Sigurd the Orkney-earl. From the
Orkney-earls it passed to the great conqueror
Godred Crovan—the King Gorry or Orry of Manx
tradition—who came from the Hebrides, and his successors down to the cession of the islands in 1266
were known as kings of Man and the Isles.

Of the details of the settlement of the Scottish mainland, of Caithness, Sutherland, and Galloway, of the occupation of Cumberland and Westmorland we know almost nothing, but when we speak later of Norse influence in these districts we shall realise how strong was their hold on them. Our knowledge of the Norse occupation of Man and the Islands is somewhat scanty in detail, but there can be no question that their settlements in lands often closely resembling in physical features their own home-country were of the highest importance.

CHAPTER VII

THE VIKINGS IN BALTIC LANDS AND RUSSIA

THE activities of the Northmen during the Viking age were not confined to the lands west and south of their original homes : the Baltic was as familiar to them as the North Sea, to go 'east-viking' was almost as common as to go 'west-viking' and Scandinavian settlements were founded on the shores of the Baltic and far inland along the great waterways leading into the heart of Russia. As was to be expected from their geographical position it was Danes and Swedes rather than Norwegians who were active in Baltic lands, the Danes settling chiefly on the Pomeranian coast among the Wends, while the Swedes occupied lands further east and founded the Scandinavian kingdom of Russia.

Already in the early years of the 9th century we find the Danish king Guðröðr now making war against his Slavonic neighbours in Mecklenburg-Schwerin, now intriguing with them against the emperor. Mention is made of more than one town on the southern coast of the Baltic bearing an essentially Scandinavian name, pointing to the existence of extensive settlements. Interesting evidence of this eastward movement is also to be found in the *Life of St Anskar*. There we learn how, soon after 830, a Danish fleet captured a city in the land of the Slavs, with great riches, and we hear in 853 how the Swedes were endeavouring to reconquer Kurland which had been under their rule, but had now thrown off the yoke and fallen a prey to a fleet of Danish Vikings—possibly the one just mentioned. St Anskar himself undertook the education of many Wendish youths who had been entrusted to him.

This and other evidence prepare us for the establishment, in the tenth century, of the most characteristic of all Viking settlements, that of Jómsborg on the Island of Wollin at the mouth of the Oder. According to tradition King Gorm the Old conquered a great kingdom in Wendland,

but it was to his son Harold Bluetooth that the
definite foundation of Jómsborg was ascribed. For
many years there had been an important trading
centre at Julin on the Island of Wollin, where
traders from Scandinavia, Saxony, Russia and many
other lands met together to take part in the rich
trade between north and south, east and west, which
passed through Julin, standing as it did on one
of the great waterways of central Europe. Large
finds of Byzantine and Arabic coins bear witness
to the extensive trade with Greece and the Orient
which passed through Julin, while the Silberberg,
on which Jómsborg once stood, is so called from
the number of silver coins from Frisia, Lorraine,
Bavaria and England which have been found there.
It was no doubt in the hope of securing some fuller
share in this trade that Harold established the great
fortress of Jómsborg and entrusted its defence to a
warrior-community on whom he imposed the strictest
rules of organisation. The story of the founding
of Jómsborg is told in the late and untrustworthy
Jómsvikingasaga, but, while we must reject many
of the details there set forth, it is probable that the
rules of the settlement as given there are based on a
genuine tradition, and they give us a vivid picture
of life in a Viking warrior-community. No one
under eighteen or over fifty years of age was
admitted to their fellowship, and neither birth nor

friendship, only personal bravery, could qualify a
man for admission. No one was allowed to continue
a member who uttered words of fear, or who fled
before one who was his equal in arms and strength.
Every member was bound to avenge a fallen
companion as if he were his brother. No women
were allowed within the community, and no one was
to be absent for more than three days without
permission. All news was to be told in the first
instance to their leader and all plunder was to be
shared at a common stake. The harbour of Jómsborg
could shelter a fleet of 300 vessels and was protected
by a mole with twelve iron gates.

The Jómsvikings played an important if stormy
part in the affairs of the three Scandinavian kingdoms
in the later years of the 10th and the early 11th
century. Many of them came to England in the
train of king Svein, while Jarl Thorkell was for a
time in the service of Ethelred the Unready. The
decline of Jómsborg as a Viking stronghold dates
from its devastation by Magnus the Good in 1043,
but the importance of Julin as a trading centre
continued unimpaired for many years to come.

From Jómsborg Harold Bluetooth's son Hákon
made an attack on Samland in the extreme east
of Prussia, but the real exploitation of the Eastern
Baltic fell as was natural to the Swedes rather than
to the Danes. We have already mentioned their

presence in Kurland on the Gulf of Riga, and we learn from Swedish runic inscriptions of expeditions to Samland, to the Semgalli (in Kurland) and to the river Duna. The important fortified port of Seeburg was probably near to Riga, while the chief trade route from the island of Gothland lay round cape Domesnæs (note the Scandinavian name) to the mouth of the Duna.

The chief work of the Swedes was however to be done in lands yet further south, in the heart of the modern empire of Russia in Europe.

The story of the founding of the Russian kingdom is preserved to us in the late 10th century chronicle of the monk Nestor, who tells us that in the year 859 'Varangians' came over the sea and took tribute from various Finnish, Tatar and Slavonic peoples inhabiting the forest regions round Lake Ilmen, between Lake Ladoga and the upper waters of the Dnieper. Again he tells us that in 862 the Varangians were driven over seas and tribute was refused, but soon the tribes quarrelled among themselves and some suggested that they should find a prince who might rule over them and keep the peace. So they sent across the sea to the Varangians, to the 'Rus,' for such is the name of these Varangians, just as others are called Swedes, Northmen, Anglians, Goths, saying that their land was great and powerful but there was no order within it and asking them to

come and rule over them. Three brothers with
their followers were chosen : the eldest, Rurik
(O.N. Hrœrekr), settled in Novgorod, the second in
Bieloözero, the third in Truvor in Izborsk. Three
years later two of the brothers died and Rurik took
control of the whole of the settlements, dividing
the land among his men. In the same year two of
Rurik's followers, Askold (O.N. Höskuldr) and Dir
(O.N. Dýri), setting out for Constantinople, halted at
Kiev and there founded a kingdom, which in 882
was conquered by Rurik's successor Oleg (O.N. Helgi)
and, as the mother of all Russian cities, became the
capital of the Russian kingdom.

There is a certain *naiveté* about this story which
is characteristic of the monkish chronicler generally,
and it is clear that, after the usual manner of the
annalist who is compiling his record long after the
events described, Nestor has grouped together
under one or two dates events which were spread
over several years, but the substantial truth of the
narrative cannot be impugned and receives abundant
confirmation from various sources.

The earliest evidence for the presence of these
' Rus' in Eastern Europe is found in the story of the
Byzantine embassy to the emperor Lewis the Pious in
839 (*v. supra*, p. 19), when certain people called 'Rhos,'
who had been on a visit to Constantinople, came in
the train of the embassy and asked leave to return

home through the empire. Enquiries were made
and it was found that these 'Rhos' were Swedes.
This would point to the presence of 'Rus' in Russia
at a date earlier than that given by Nestor, and
indeed the rapid extension of their influence indicates
a period of activity considerably longer than that
allowed by him. These 'Rus' or 'Rhos' soon came
into relations, both of trade and war, with the
Byzantine empire. We have preserved to us from
the years 911 and 944 commercial treaties made
between the 'Rus' and the Greeks showing that
they brought all kinds of furs and also slaves to
Constantinople, receiving in exchange various articles
of luxury including gold and silver ornaments, silks
and other rich stuffs. The names of the signatories
to these treaties are, on the side of the 'Rus,' almost
entirely of Scandinavian origin and may to some
extent be shown to be of definitely Swedish
provenance. About the year 950, the emperor
Constantine Porphyrogenitus, writing a tractate on
the administration of the empire, describes how
traders from various parts of Russia assemble at
Kiev and sail down the Dnieper on their way to
Constantinople. Their course down the Dnieper was
impeded by a series of rapids, and Constantine gives
their names both in 'Russian' and in Slavonic form,
and though the names are extremely corrupt in
their Greek transcription there is no mistaking that

the 'Russian' names are really forms belonging to
some Scandinavian dialect.

The Rus were also well known as warriors and
raiders.   In 865 they sailed down the Dnieper,
across the Black Sea and made their way into the
Sea of Marmora. Their fleet was dispersed by a
storm, but they were more successful in 907 when
Oleg with some 2000 ships harried the environs
of Constantinople and was bought off by a heavy
tribute. These attacks were continued at intervals
during the next century.

We also find a good deal of interesting information
about these 'Rûs,' as they are called, in various Arab
historians. We hear how they sailed their vessels
down the chief waterways and had such a firm hold
on the Black Sea that by the year 900 it was already
known as the Russian Sea.   Often they dragged their
vessels overland from one stream to another, and
thus they made their way from the upper waters
of the Don down the Volga to the Caspian Sea.
But not only do we have a description of their
journeyings we also learn a good deal of their
customs and habits, and, though at times the information given is open to suspicion, archaeological research
tends to confirm the statements of these historians
and to show that the civilisation of the 'Rûs' closely
resembled that of the Scandinavian peoples generally
in the Viking age.

The identification of the ancient 'Rus' with the Swedes was long and hotly contested by Slavonic patriots but there is now a general consensus of opinion that the evidence for it is too strong to be overthrown. Not only have we the evidence given above but also the very names 'Rus' and 'Varangian' can be satisfactorily explained only on this theory. The name 'Rus' is the Slavonic, 'Rhôs' the Greek, and 'Rûs' the Arabic form of the Finnish name for Sweden, viz. Ruotsi. This name was originally derived from *Roþr* or *Roþin*, the name of certain districts of Upland and Östergötland, whose inhabitants were known as *Rods-karlar* or *Rods-mœn*. The Finns had early come into relation with the Swedes and they used the name of those people with whom they were in earliest and most intimate contact for the whole Swedish nationality. When these Swedes settled in Russia the Finns applied the same term to the new colonists and the term came to be adopted later into the various Slavonic dialects.

We are most familiar with the term 'Varangian' or 'Variag,' to use the Slavonic form, as applied to the famous guard of the Byzantine emperors, which seems to have been formed in the latter half of the 10th century and was largely composed of Norwegian, Icelandic and Swedish recruits. In Russian and Arabic historians on the other hand the term is used rather in an ethnographic or geographic sense.

We have seen that it was thus used by Nestor, and similarly we find the Baltic commonly spoken of as the 'Varangian' Sea both in Russian and in Arabic records. All the evidence tends to show that this was the earlier sense of the term and we find it gradually displacing the term 'Rhôs' even in Byzantine historians. The word itself is of Scandinavian origin and means 'those who are bound together by a pledge.' The theory which best explains its various uses is that put forward by Dr Vilhelm Thomsen, viz. that it originated among the Northmen who settled in Russia, i.e. among the ancient Russ, and that under that term they denoted those peoples west of the Baltic who were related to them by nationality.

From the Russ the word passed into the Slavonic language as *variag*[1], into the Greek as *barangoi*—where it was often used in the restricted sense of members of the imperial guard largely recruited from this nation,—and into the Arabic as *varank*. Dr Thomsen adduces two happy parallels for the somewhat remarkable history of the terms 'Russian' and 'Varangian.' The term 'Russian' came to be used as their own name by the Slavonic peoples, who were once ruled over by the Russ, in much the same way that the term 'Frankish' or 'French' was adopted by the Gaulish population of France from

[1] The word *variag* in Modern Russian means a pedlar and bears witness to the strong commercial instincts of the Viking.

its Germanic conquerors. The term 'Varangian,' ultimately the name for a nation or group of nations, came to be used of a military force once largely recruited from those nations, much in the same way as the term 'Swiss' was applied to the Papal guard long after that guard had ceased to be recruited from the Swiss nation exclusively.

The belief in the Scandinavian origin of the Russ is amply supported by archaeological evidence. The large number of Arabic coins found in Sweden (more especially in Gothland) and in Russia itself points to an extensive trade with the Orient whose route lay chiefly to the east of the Caspian Sea and then along the valley of the Volga. The dates of the coins point to the years between 850 and 1000 as those of most active intercourse with the East. Equally interesting is the large number of western coins, more especially Anglo-Saxon pennies and sceatts, which have been found in Russia. They probably represent portions of our Danegeld which had come into the hands of the Swedes either in trade or war. Viking brooches of the characteristic oval shape with the familiar zoomorphic ornamentation have been found in Western Russia, and one stone with a runic inscription, belonging to the 11th century and showing evidence of connexion with Gothland, has been found in a burial mound in Berezan, an island at the mouth of the Dnieper.

Professor Braun says that no others have been found because of the rarity of suitable stone.

How long the Russ maintained their distinctively Scandinavian nationality it is difficult to determine. Oleg's grandson Svjatoslav bore a distinctively Slavonic name, and henceforward the names of the members of the royal house are uniformly Slavonic, but the connexion with Sweden was by no means forgotten. Svjatoslav's son Vladimir the Great secured himself in the rulership of Novgorod in 980 by the aid of *variags* from over the sea and established a band of variag warriors in his chief city of Kiev. But the Viking age was drawing to a close. Variag auxiliaries are mentioned for the last time in 1043 and it is probable that by the middle of the 11th century the Scandinavian settlers had been almost completely Slavonicised. Of their permanent influence on the Russian people and on Russian institutions it is, in the present state of our knowledge, almost impossible to speak. Attempts have been made to distinguish Scandinavian elements in the old Russian law and language but with no very definite results, and we must content ourselves with the knowledge that the Vikings were all powerful in Western and Southern Russia during the greater part of two centuries, carrying on an extensive trade with the East, establishing Novgorod, 'the new town,' on the Volga under the name *Holmgarðr* and founding a dynasty which ruled in Kiev and became a considerable power in eastern Europe negotiating on terms of equality with the Byzantine emperors.

Mention has already been made more than once of the way in which the Northmen entered the service of the emperors at Constantinople or *Miklagarðr*, 'the great city,' as they called it. From here they visited all parts of the Mediterranean. When Harold Hardrada was in the service of the emperor he sailed through the Grecian archipelago to Sicily and Africa. There he stayed several years, conquering some eighty cities for his master and gaining rich treasures for himself. One interesting memorial of these journeys still remains to us. At the entrance to the arsenal in Venice stands a marble lion brought from Athens in 1687. Formerly it stood at the harbour of the Piraeus, known thence as the Porto Leone. On the sides of the lion are carved two long runic inscriptions arranged in snake-like bands. The runes are too much worn to be deciphered but they are unquestionably of Scandinavian origin and the snake-bands closely resemble those that may be seen on certain runic stones in Sweden. The carving was probably done by Swedes from Uppland about the middle of the 10th century. One can hardly imagine a more striking illustration of the extent and importance of the Viking movement in Europe.

M.   6

CHAPTER VIII

VIKING CIVILISATION

THE activities of the Vikings were all-embracing, and before any attempt can be made to estimate their influence in the various countries which came permanently under their rule, or were brought more or less closely into touch with them, some account, however slight, must be given of Scandinavian civilisation at this time, both on its spiritual and on its material sides. For the former aspect we must turn chiefly to the poems and sagas of old Norse literature, for the latter to the results of modern archaeological research. So far as the poems and sagas are concerned it is well to remember that they were to a large extent composed in Iceland and reflect the somewhat peculiar type of civilisation developed there at a period just subsequent to the Viking age itself. This civilisation differs necessarily from that developed in Scandinavia or in the other Scandinavian settlements, in that it was free from Western influence, but this is to some extent compensated for by the fact that we get in Iceland a better picture of the inherent possibilities of Viking civilisation when developed on independent lines.

At the beginning of the Viking age the Scandinavian peoples were in a transitional stage of
development ; on the one hand there was still much,
both in their theory and in their practice of life, that
savoured of primitive barbarism, while on the other,
in the development of certain phases of human
activity, more especially in those of war, trade, and
social organisation, they were considerably ahead
of many of their European neighbours.   More than
one writer has commented upon the strange blending
of barbarism and culture which constitutes Viking
civilisation: it is evident when we study their
daily life, and it is emphasised in the story of
their slow and halting passage from heathenism to
Christianity.

We need not travel far to find examples of their
barbarism.   Their cruelty in warfare is a common-
place among the historians of the period.   When the
Irish found the Danes cooking their food on spits
stuck in the bodies of their fallen foes (*v. supra*,
p. 55) and asked why they did anything so hateful,
the answer came 'Why not ?   If the other side had
been victorious they would have done the same with
us.'   The custom of cutting the blood-eagle (i.e.
cutting the ribs in the shape of an eagle and pulling
the lungs through the opening) was a well-known
form of vengeance taken on the slayer of one's father
if captured in battle, and is illustrated in the story

6—2

of the sons of Ragnarr Loðbrók himself. Another survival of primitive life was the famous Berserk fury, when men in the heat of battle were seized with sudden madness and, according to the popular belief, received a double portion of strength, and lost all sense of bodily pain, a custom for which Dr Bugge finds an apt parallel in the 'running amok' of the races of the Malay peninsula. Children were tossed on the point of the spear and the Viking leader who discouraged the custom was nicknamed *barnakarl*, i.e. children's friend.

In contrast to these methods of warfare stands their skill in fortification, in which they taught many lessons both to their English and to their Frankish adversaries, their readiness in adapting themselves to new conditions of warfare (*v. supra*, p. 46), and their clever strategy, whereby they again and again outwitted their opponents.

The same contrast meets us when we consider the position of women among them. The chroniclers make many references to their lust after women. We hear in an English chronicler how they combed their hair, indulged in sabbath baths, often changed their clothes and in various ways cultivated bodily beauty 'in order that they might the more readily overcome the chastity of the matrons, and make concubines even of the daughters of the nobility.' Wandering from country to country they often had

wives in each, and polygamy would seem to have
been the rule, at least among the leaders. In Ireland
we hear of what seem to have been veritable harems,
while in Russia we are told of the great grandson
of Rurik, the founder of the Russian kingdom, that
he had more than 800 concubines, though we may
perhaps suspect the influence of Oriental custom in
this case. Yet, side by side with all this, the legitimate
wife was esteemed and honoured, and attained a
position and took a part in national life which was
quite unusual in those days. In the account of an
Arabic embassy to the Vikings of the west (*v. supra*,
p. 20) we have a vivid picture of the freedom of
their married life. Auðr, the widow of Olaf the
White, after the fall of her son Thorstein, took
charge of the fortunes of her family and is one
of the figures that stand out most clearly in the
early settlement of Iceland. We have only to turn
to the Icelandic sagas to see before us a whole
gallery of portraits, dark and fair alike, of women
cast in heroic mould, while the stone at Dyrna in
Hadeland, bearing the runic inscription, 'Gunvor,
daughter of Thirek, built a bridge to commemorate
her daughter Astrid, she was the most gracious
maiden in Hadeland,' gives us one of the most attractive pictures of womanhood left to us from the Viking
age. It must be added however that beside the
runic inscription, the stone bears carvings of the

Christ-child, the star in the east and the three kings, and this may serve to remind us that the age was one in which the peoples of the North passed from heathenism to Christianity, though the passage was a slow one and by no means complete even at the close of the period.

It is probable that the first real knowledge of 'the white Christ' came, as is so often the case, with the extension of trade—Frisians trading with Scandinavia, and Danes and Swedes settling in Frisia and elsewhere for the same purpose. St Willibrord at the beginning of the 8th century and Archbishop Ebbo of Rheims in 823, as papal legate among the northern peoples, undertook missions to Denmark, but it was in 826, when king Harold was baptised at Mainz, that the first real opportunity came for the preaching of Christianity in Denmark. Harold was accompanied on his return by St Anskar, a monk from Corvey and a man filled with religious zeal. After two years' mission in Denmark St Anskar sailed to Sweden, where he was graciously received at Björkö by king Björn. He made many converts and on his return home in 831 was made archbishop of Hamburg and given, jointly with Ebbo, jurisdiction over the whole of the northern realms. Hamburg was devastated in 845 and St Anskar was then appointed to the bishopric of Bremen, afterwards united to a restored archbishopric of Hamburg. He laboured in Denmark once more and established churches at Slesvík and Ribe. He conducted a second mission to Sweden and his missionary zeal remained unabated until his death in 865 ; his work was carried on by his successor and biographer St Rimbert and by many others. Their preaching was however confined to Jutland and South Sweden and there is no evidence of any popular movement towards Christianity. Gorm the Old was a steadfast pagan but Gorm's son Harold Bluetooth was a zealous promoter of Christianity. His enthusiasm may have been exaggerated by monastic chroniclers in contrast to the heathenism of his son Svein, but with the accession of Cnut all fears of a reversion to heathendom were at an end. Cnut was a devout son of the Church.

The first Danish settlers in England were entirely heathen in sentiment, but they were soon brought into close contact with Christianity, and the terms of the peace of Edward and Guthrum in the early years of the 10th century show that already Christianity was making its way in the Danelagh. In the course of this century both archbishoprics were held by men of Danish descent and the excesses of the early 11th century were due, not to the Danish settlers, but to the heathen followers of Olaf Tryggvason and Svein Forkbeard. Similarly the Danish settlers in Normandy were within a few years numbered among the Church's most enthusiastic supporters, and Rollo's own son and successor William was anxious to become a monk.

The story of the preaching of Christianity in Norway is a chequered one. The first attempt to establish the Christian faith was made by Hákon Aðalsteinsfóstri (*v. supra*, p. 36). Baptised and educated in England, he began warily, inducing those who were best beloved by him to become Christians, but he soon came into conflict with the more ardent followers of paganism. At the great autumn festival at Lade when the cups of memory were drunk, Earl Sigurd signed a cup to Odin, but the king made the sign of the cross over his cup. Earl Sigurd pacified popular clamour by saying that the king had made the sign of the hammer and consecrated the cup to Thor. The next day the king would not eat the horse-flesh used in their offerings nor drink the blood from it : the people were angry and the king compromised by inhaling the steam from the offering through a linen cloth placed over the sacrificial kettle, but no one was satisfied and at the next winter-feast the king had to eat some bits of horse-liver and to drink crossless all the cups of memory. Hákon died a Christian but Eyvindr Skaldaspillir in *Hákonarmál* describes how he was welcomed by Odin to Valhalla.

Earl Hákon Sigurdson, nicknamed *blót-jarl*, i.e.

sacrifice-earl, was a zealous heathen, but Olaf Trygg-vason after his succession in 995 promoted the cause of Christianity by every means in his power, and it was largely to this that he owed his ultimate overthrow. Then, after a brief interval, the crown passed to St Olaf, greatest of all Christian champions in Norway, and during his reign that country became definitely Christian, though his rough and ready methods of conversion were hardly likely to secure anything but a purely formal and outward adhesion to the new faith.

Sweden was the most reluctant of the three northern realms to accept Christianity, and the country remained almost entirely heathen until the close of the Viking period.

The story of the Norse settlers in Ireland and the Western Islands in their relation to Christianity was very much that of the Danes in England. Celtic Christianity had a firm hold in these countries, and from the earliest period of the settlements many of the Vikings adopted the Christian faith. Among the settlers in Iceland who came from the West were many Christians, and Auðr herself gave orders at her death that she should be buried on the sea-shore below the tide-mark, rather than lie in unhallowed ground. Most of the settlers undoubtedly remained heathen—in 996 a ring sacred to Thor was taken from a temple in Dublin and in 1000 king Brian

destroyed a grove sacred to the same god just north
of the city. But side by side with incidents of this
kind must be placed others like that of the sparing
of the churches, hospitals and almshouses when
Armagh was sacked in 921, or the retirement
of Anlaf Cuaran to the monastery at Iona in 981.
In Ireland as elsewhere there seems to have been a
recrudescence of heathenism in the early years of
the 11th century and the great fight at Clontarf
was regarded as a struggle between pagan and
Christian.

Outwardly the Scandinavian world had largely
declared its adhesion to Christianity by the close
of the Viking period, but we must remember that
the medieval Church was satisfied if her converts
passed through the ceremony of baptism and observed
her rites, though their sentiments often remained
heathen. Except in purely formal fashion it is
impossible to draw a definite line of demarcation
between Christian and heathen, and the acceptance
of Christianity is of importance not so much from
any change of outlook which it produced in in-
dividuals, as because it brought the peoples of the
North into closer touch with the general life and
culture of medieval Europe. Leaders freely accepted
baptism—often more than once—and even confirmation as part of a diplomatic bargain, while their
profession of Christianity made no difference to their

Viking way of life. Even on formal lines the Church had to admit of compromise, as for example in the practice of *prime-signing*, whereby when Vikings visited Christian lands as traders, or entered the service of Christian kings for payment, they often allowed themselves to be signed with the cross, which secured their admission to intercourse with Christian communities, but left them free to hold the faith which pleased them best.

Strange forms and mixtures of belief arose in the passage from one faith to the other. Helgi the Lean was a Christian, but called on Thor in the hour of need. The Christian saints with their wonder-working powers were readily adopted into the Norse Pantheon, and Vikings by their prayers and offerings secured the help of St Patrick in Ireland and of St Germanus in France in times of defeat and pestilence, while we hear of a family of settlers in Iceland who gave up all faith except a belief in the power of St Columba. On sculptured stones in the west may be found pictures of Ragnarök, of Balder and of Loki together with the sign of the cross. Some of the heathen myths themselves show Christian influence; the Balder story with its echoes of the lamentations for the suffering Christ belongs to the last stage of Norse heathendom, while a heathen skald makes Christ sit by the Fountain of Fate as the mighty destroyer of the giants. When

the virtue had gone out of their old beliefs many
fell a prey to the grossest superstition, worshipping
the rocks and groves and rivers once thought to be
the dwelling place of the gods. Others renounced
faith in Christian and heathen gods alike, and the
nickname 'godless' is by no means rare among the
settlers in Iceland. Of such it is often said that
they believed in themselves, or had no faith in aught
except their own strength and power, while in the
saga of Friþjof we hear how the hero paid little
heed to the sanctity of the temple of Balder and
that the love of Ingibjorg meant more to him than
the wrath of the gods. For a parallel to such
audacious scepticism as that of Friþjof we must
turn to southern lands and later times with Aucassin's
'In Paradise what have I to win? Therein I seek not
to enter, but only to have my Nicolete, my sweet
lady that I love so well.' For some the way of
escape came not by superstition or by scepticism,
but in mystic speculation, in pure worship of the
powers of nature. Thus we hear of the Icelander
Thorkell Mani, whom all praised for the excellence
of his way of life, that in his last illness he was
carried out into the sunshine, so that he might
commend himself into the hands of the god who
made the sun, or of the goði Askell who, even in the
hour of famine, deemed it was more fitting to honour
the creator by caring for the aged and the children,

than to relieve distress by putting these helpless ones
to death.

One other illustration of the declining force
of heathenism must be mentioned. It is to the
Viking age that we owe the poems of the older Edda,
that storehouse of Norse mythology and cosmogony.
They are almost purely heathen in sentiment, and
yet one feels that it could only be in an age when
belief in the old gods was passing away that the
authors of these poems could have struck those
notes of detachment, irony, and even of burlesque,
which characterise so many of them.

The condition of faith and belief in the Viking
age was, then, chaotic, but, fortunately for purposes
of clear statement, there was, to the Norse mind
at least, no necessary connexion between beliefs and
morality, between faith and conduct, and the ideas
on which they based their philosophy and practice
of life are fairly distinct.

The central ideas which dominate the Norse view
of life are an ever-present sense of the passingness
of all things and a deep consciousness of the
over-ruling power of Fate. All earthly things are
transitory and the one thing which lasts is good
fame. 'Wealth dies, kinsmen die, man himself must
die, but the fame which a man wins rightly for
himself never dies ; one thing I know that never
dies, the judgment passed on every man that dies,'

says the poet of the *Hávamál*, the great storehouse of the gnomic wisdom of the Norsemen. 'All things are unstable and transitory, let no man therefore be arrogant or over-confident. The wise man will never praise the day before it is evening.' Prudence and foresight are ever necessary. All things are determined by a fate which is irrevocable and cannot be avoided. Every man must die the death that is appointed for him, and the man whose final day has not yet come may face unmoved the greatest danger. This sense of an inevitable fate must lead to no weakening of character or weariness of life. Death must be faced with cheerful stoicism and our judgment of the worth of any man must depend on the way in which he awaits the decree of fate. Place no great trust in others whether friend or foe, least of all place trust in women. 'Wommennes conseils been ful ofte colde,' says Chaucer in the *Nun's Priest's Tale*, using an old Scandinavian proverb. 'Be friendly to your friends and a foeman to your foes. Practice hospitality and hate lying and untruthfulness.' With their enemies the Vikings had an evil reputation for cunning and deceit, but when we study the incidents on which this charge was based—as for example the story of the capture of Luna (*v. supra*, p. 47) or the oft-repeated trick of feigning flight, only to lure the enemy away from safe ground—one must confess that they show an

enemy outwitted rather than deceived. This aspect
of Viking character perhaps finds its best illustration
in the figure of Odin. His common epithets are
'the wise,' 'the prudent,' 'the sagacious'; he is a
god of witchcraft and knows all the secret powers
of nature and stands in contrast to the simple-minded
Thor, endowed with mighty strength, but less polished
and refined. The development of the worship of
Odin in Norway belongs specially to the later
Iron Age, and it is worthy of note that his worship
seems to have prevailed chiefly in military circles,
among princes and their retainers.

The Vikings were guilty of two besetting sins—
immoderate love of wine and of women. Of their
relations to women enough has been said already.
Their drunken revelry is best illustrated by the story
of the orgie which led up to the death of St Alphege
in London in 1012, when, after drinking their fill
of the wine they had brought from abroad, they
pelted the bishop with bones from the feast, and
finally pierced his skull with the spike on the back
of an axe. Of sin in the Christian sense the Vikings
had no conception. An Irish chronicler tells us
indeed that the Danes have a certain piety in that
they can refrain from flesh and from women for a
time, but a truer description is probably that given
by Adam of Bremen when he says that the Danes
can weep neither for their sins nor for their dead.

The chief occupations of the Vikings were trade
and war, but we must beware of drawing a too rigid
distinction between adventurers and peaceful stay-at-
homes. The Vikings when they settled in England
and elsewhere showed that their previous roving life
did not hinder them in the least from settling down
as peaceful traders, farmers, or peasant-labourers,
while the figure of Ohthere or Óttarr, to give him his
Norse name, who entered the service of king Alfred,
may serve to remind us that many a landed gentleman
was not above carrying on a good trade with the
Finns or undertaking voyages of exploration in the
White Sea.

Trading in those days was a matter of great
difficulty and many risks. The line of division
between merchant and Viking was a very thin one,
and more than once we read how, when merchants
went on a trading expedition, they arranged a truce
until their business was concluded and then treated
each other as enemies. Trade in Scandinavia was
carried on either in fixed centres or in periodical
markets held in convenient places. The chief trading
centres were the twin towns of Slesvík-Hedeby in
Denmark, Skiringssalr in S.W. Norway, and Björkö,
Sigtuna and the island of Gothland in Sweden, while
an important market was held periodically at Bohuslän
on the Götaelv, at a place were the boundaries of
the three northern kingdoms met. A characteristic

incident which happened at this market illustrates
the international character of the trade done there.
On a certain occasion a wealthy merchant named
Gille (the name is Celtic), surnamed the Russian
because of his many journeys to that country, set
up his booth in the market and received a visit from
the Icelander Höskuldr who was anxious to buy
a female slave. Gille drew back a curtain dividing
off the inner part of the tent and showed Höskuldr
twelve female slaves. Höskuldr bought one and
she proved to be an Irish king's daughter who had
been made captive by Viking raiders.

The chief exports were furs, horses, wool, and fish
while the imports consisted chiefly in articles of
luxury, whether for clothing or ornament. There
was an extensive trade with the Orient in all such
luxuries and the Vikings seem eagerly to have
accumulated wealth of this kind. When Limerick
was re-captured by the Irish in 968, they carried
off from the Vikings 'their jewels and their best
property, and their saddles beautiful and foreign
(probably of Spanish workmanship), their gold and
their silver: their beautifully woven cloth of all
colours and all kinds: their satins and silken cloths,
pleasing and variegated, both scarlet and green, and
all sorts of cloth in like manner.' They captured
too 'their soft, youthful, bright, matchless girls:
their blooming silk-clad young women: and their

active, large, and well formed boys.' Such captives
whether made by Irish from Norsemen or Norsemen
from Irish would certainly be sold as slaves, for one
of the chief branches of trade in those days was the
sale as slaves of those made prisoner in war.

The expansion of Scandinavian trade took place
side by side with, rather than as a result of, Viking
activity in war. There is evidence of the presence
of traders in the Low Country early in the 9th century,
and already in the days of St Anskar we hear of a
Swedish widow of Björkö who left money for her
daughter to distribute among the poor of Duurstede.
Jómsborg was established to protect and increase
Scandinavian trade at Julin, and there were other
similar trading centres on the southern and eastern
shores of the Baltic.

The Viking might busy himself either with war
or trade, but whatever his occupation, living as he
did in insular or peninsular lands, good ships and
good seamanship were essential to his livelihood.
Seamen now often abandoned that timid hugging
of the coast, sailing only by day time and in fair
weather, which characterised the old Phoenician
traders, and boldly sailed across the uncharted main
with no help save that of the sun and stars by which
to steer their course. It was this boldness of spirit
alone which enabled them to reach the lonely Faroes,
the distant Shetlands and Orkneys, and the yet more

remote Iceland. Irish monks and anchorites had
shown similar fearlessness, but their bravery was
often that of the fanatic and the mystic rather than
the enterprise of the seaman. Boldness of seamanship led to boldness in exploration. From Iceland
the Vikings sailed to Greenland, and by the year
1000 had discovered Vinland, the N.E. part of
North America. Ottarr rounded the North Cape
and sailed the White Sea in the 9th century, while
Harold Hardrada in the 11th century made a voyage
of Polar exploration.

Of their ships we know a good deal both from the
sagas and from the remains of actual ships preserved
to us. The custom of ship-burial, i.e. burial in a ship
over which a grave chamber, covered with a how or
mound, was erected, was common in the Viking age,
and several such ships have been discovered. The
two most famous are those of Gokstad and Oseberg,
both found on the shores of Christiania Fjord.
The Gokstad vessel is of oak, clinker-built, with seats
for sixteen pairs of rowers, and is 28 ft. long and 16 ft.
broad amidships. It dates from about 900, and in
form and workmanship is not surpassed by modern
vessels of a similar kind. There is a mast for a
single sail, and the rudder, as always in those days,
is on the starboard side. The gunwale was decorated
with a series of shields painted alternately black
and gold. The appearance of the vessel when fully

7—2

equipped can perhaps best be judged from the pictures of Viking ships to be seen in the Bayeux tapestry. There we may note the parti-coloured sail with its variegated stripes, and the rich carving of stem and stern. These magnificent sails were a source of much pride to their possessors, and the story is told of Sigurd Jerusalem-farer that on his way home from Jerusalem to Constantinople he lay for half-a-month off Cape Malea, waiting for a side wind, so that his sails might be set lengthwise along the ship and so be better seen by those standing on shore as he sailed up to Constantinople. The stem often ended in a dragon's head done over with gold, whilst the stern was frequently shaped like a dragon's tail, so that the vessel itself was often called a dragon.

The Oseberg ship is of a different type. The gunwale is lower and the whole vessel is flatter and broader. It is used as the grave-chamber of a woman, and the whole appearance of the vessel, including its richly carved stem, indicates that it was used in calm waters for peaceful purposes.

The story of the escape of Hárek of Thjotta through Copenhagen Sound after the battle of Helgeää in 1018 illustrates the difference between a trading-ship and a ship of war. Hárek struck sail and mast, took down the vane, stretched a grey tent-cloth over the ship's sides, and left only a few rowers fore and aft. The rest of the crew were

PLATE I

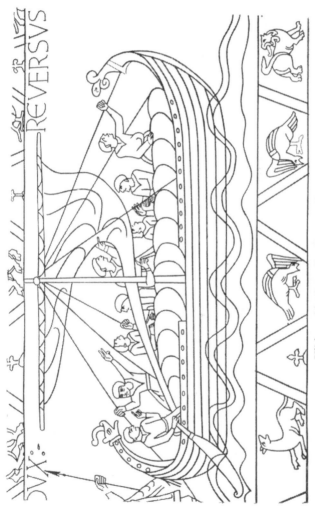

Viking ship from the Bayeux Tapestry

bidden lie flat so that they might not be seen, with the result that the Danes mistook Hárek's war-galley for a trading-vessel laden with herrings or salt and let it pass unchallenged.

In the last years of the Viking period ships increased greatly both in size and number. Olaf Tryggvason's vessel, the *Long Serpent*, in which he fought his last fight at Svoldr, had thirty benches of oars, while Cnut the Great had one with sixty pairs of oars. This same king went with a fleet of some fourteen hundred vessels to the conquest of Norway.

In battle the weapons of defence were helmet, corselet and shield. The shields were of wood with a heavy iron boss in the centre. The corselets were made of iron rings, leather, or thick cloth. The weapons of offence were mainly sword, spear and battle-axe. The sword was of the two-edged type and usually had a shallow depression along the middle of the blade, known as the blood-channel. Above, the blade terminated in a narrow tang, bounded at either end by the hilts. Round the tang and between the hilts was the handle of wood, horn, or some similar material, often covered with leather, or occasionally with metal. Above the upper hilt was a knob, which gave the sword the necessary balance for a good steady blow. Generally the knob and the hilts were inlaid with silver, bronze, or copper-work. The battle-axe, the most characteristic of Viking weapons, was of the heavy broad-bladed type.

Next to warfare and trade, the chief occupation of the Viking was farming, while his chief amusement was the chase. At home the Viking leader lived the life of an active country gentleman. His favourite sport was hawking, and one of the legendary lives of St Edmund tells how Ragnarr Loðbrók himself was driven by stress of storm to land on the East Anglian coast, receiving a hospitable welcome from the king, but ultimately meeting death at the hands of the king's huntsman who was jealous of his prowess as a fowler.

Of the social organisation of the Vikings it is impossible to form a very definite or precise picture. We have in the laws of the Jómsborg settlement (*v. supra*, p. 71) the rule of life of a warrior-community, but it would be a mistake to imagine that these laws prevailed in all settlements alike. The general structure of their society was aristocratic rather than democratic, but within the aristocracy, which was primarily a military one, the principle of equality prevailed. When asked who was their lord, Rollo's men answered 'We have no lord, we are all equal.' But while they admitted no lord, the Vikings were essentially practical; they realised the importance of organised leadership, and we have a succession of able leaders mentioned in the annals

of the time, to some of whom the title king was
given. These kings however are too numerous, and
too many of them are mentioned together, for it to
be possible to give the term king in this connexion
anything like its usual connotation. It would seem
rather to have been used for any prince of the royal
house, and it was only when the Vikings had formed
fixed settlements and come definitely under Western
influence that we hear of kings in the ordinary
territorial sense—kings of Northumbria, Dublin, Man
and the Isles, or East Anglia. We hear also of *jarls*
or earls, either as Viking leaders or as definite
territorial rulers, as for example the Orkney-earls
and more than one earl who is mentioned as ruling
in Dublin, but these earls usually held their lands
under the authority of a king. By the side of kings
and earls mention is made both in the Danelagh
and also in the Western Islands of *lawmen*. It is
difficult exactly to define their position and function.
Originally these men were simply experts in the law
who expounded it in the popular *thing* or assembly,
and were the spokesmen of the people as against
the king and the court, but sometimes they assumed
judicial functions, acting for example in Sweden as
assessors to the king, who was supreme judge.

In their home life we find the same strange
mixture of civilisation and barbarism which marks
them elsewhere. Their houses were built of timber,

covered with clay. There was no proper hearth and
the smoke from the fire made its way out as best
it could through the turf-covered roof. The chief
furniture of the room consisted in beds, benches,
long tables and chests, and in the houses of the rich
these would at the close of our period often be
carved with stories from the old heroic or mythologic
legends, while the walls might be covered with
tapestry. Prominent in the chieftain's hall stood the
carved pillars which supported his high-seat and
were considered sacred. When some of the settlers
first sailed to Iceland they threw overboard their
high-seat pillars which they had brought with them,
and chose as the site of their new abode the place
where these pillars were cast ashore.

In clothing and adornment there can be no
question that our Viking forefathers had attained
a high standard of luxury. Any visitor to the great
national museums at Copenhagen, Stockholm or
Christiania must be impressed by the wealth of
personal ornaments displayed before him: magnificent
brooches of silver and bronze, arm-rings and neck-
rings of gold and silver, large beads of silver, glass,
rock-crystal, amber and cornelian. At one time it
was commonly assumed that these ornaments, often
displaying the highest artistic skill, were simply
plunder taken by the Vikings from nations more
cultured and artistic than themselves, but patient

PLATE II

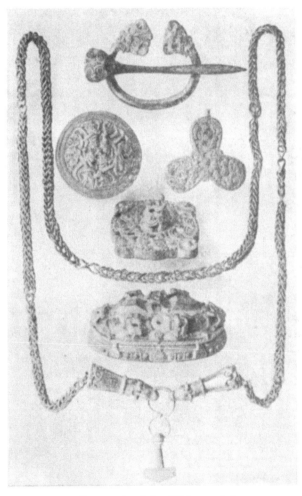

Ornaments of the Viking period

investigation has shown that the majority of them were wrought in Scandinavia itself.

The most characteristic of Viking ornaments is undoubtedly the brooch. It was usually oval in shape and the concave surface was covered with a framework of knobs and connecting bands, which divided it into a series of 'fields' (to use a heraldic term), which could themselves be decorated with the characteristic ornamentation of the period. The commonest form of oval brooch was that with nine knobs on a single plate, but in the later examples the plate is often doubled. The brooches themselves were of bronze, the knobs usually of silver with silver wire along the edge of the brooch. These knobs have now often disappeared and the bronze has become dull with verdigris, so that it is difficult to form an idea of their original magnificence. The oval brooches were used to fasten the outer mantle and were usually worn in pairs, either on the breast or on the shoulders, and examples of them have been found from Russia in the East to Ireland on the West. Other types of brooch are also found— straight-armed, trilobed and round. Such brooches were often worn in the middle of the bosom a little below the oval ones. Other ornaments beside brooches are common—arm-rings, neck-rings, pendants. One of the most interesting of the pendants is a ring with a series of small silver Thor's hammers which was probably used as a charm against ill-luck. All these ornaments alike are in silver rather than gold, and it has been said that if the post-Roman period of Scandinavian archaeology be called the age of Gold, the Viking period should be named the age of Silver.

The style of ornamentation used in these articles of personal adornment as well as in objects of more general use, such as horse-trappings, is that commonly known to German archaeologists as *tier-ornamentik*, i.e. animal or zoomorphic ornamentation. This last translation may sound pedantic but it is the most accurate description of the style, for we have no attempt to represent the full form of any animal that ever had actual existence; rather we find the various limbs of animals—heads, legs, tails—woven into one another in fantastic design in order to cover a certain surface-area which requires decoration. 'The animals are ornaments and treated as such. They are stretched and curved, lengthened and shortened, refashioned, and remodelled just as the space which they must fill requires.' This style was once called the 'dragon-style,' but the term is misleading as there is no example belonging to the Viking period proper of any attempt to represent a dragon, i.e. some fantastic animal with wings. Such creatures belong to a later period.

The zoomorphic style did not have its origin

during the Viking period. It is based on that
of a preceding period in the culture of the North
German peoples, but it received certain characteristic
developments at this time, more especially under the
influence of Irish and Frankish art. Irish art had
begun to influence that of Scandinavia even before
the Viking period began, and the development
of intercourse between North and West greatly
strengthened that influence. To Frankish influence
were due not only certain developments of *tier-
ornamentik* but also the use of figures from the
plant-world for decorative purposes. One of the
finest brooches preserved to us from this period is
of Frankish workmanship—a magnificent trilobed
brooch of gold with acanthus-leaf ornamentation.
This leaf-work was often imitated by Scandinavian
craftsmen but the imitation is usually rude and
unconvincing. Traces are also to be found of Oriental
and more especially of Arabic influence in certain
forms of silver-ornamentation, but finds of articles
of actual Eastern manufacture are more common
than finds of articles of Scandinavian origin showing
Eastern influences in their workmanship.

Buried treasure from the Viking period is very
common. It was a popular belief, sanctioned by the
express statement of Odin, that a man would enjoy
in Valhalla whatsoever he had himself buried in
the earth. Another common motive in the burial of

treasure was doubtless the desire to find a place
of security against robbery and plunder. Treasure
thus secreted would often be lost sight of at the
owner's death. To the burial-customs of the Viking
period also we owe much of our knowledge of their
weapons, clothing, ornaments and even of their
domestic utensils.

The dead were as a rule cremated, at least during
the earlier part of the Viking period. The body
burned or unburned was either buried in a mound
of earth, forming a 'how,' or was laid under the
surface of the ground, and the grave marked by
stones arranged in a circle, square, triangle or oval,
sometimes even imitating the outlines of a ship.
The 'hows' were often of huge size. The largest
of the three 'King's hows' at Old Upsala is 30 ft.
high and 200 ft. broad. A large how was very
necessary in the well-known ship-burial when the
dead man (or woman) was placed in a grave-chamber
on board his ship and the ship was drawn on land
and buried within a how. Men and women alike
were buried in full dress, and the men usually have
all their weapons with them. In the latter case
weapons tend to take the place of articles of domestic
use such as are found in the graves of an earlier
period, and the change points to a new conception
of the future life. It is now a life in which warriors
feast with Odin in Valhalla on benches that are

covered with corselets. A careful examination of
Norwegian graves has proved fairly definitely the
existence of the custom of 'suttee' during the Viking
period, and the evidence of the Arab historian
Ibn Fadhlan seems to show that the same custom
prevailed among the Rûs. Horses, dogs, hawks and
other animals were often buried with their masters,
and the remains of such, burned or unburned, have
frequently been found.

The varying customs attending burial are happily
illustrated in the two accounts preserved to us
of the burial of king Harold Hyldetan, who died
c. 750. The accounts were written down long after
the actual event, but they probably give us a good
picture of familiar incidents in burial ceremonies
of the Viking period.

One account (in a late saga) tells how, on the
morrow of the great fight at Bravalla, king Ring
caused search to be made for the body of his kinsman
Harold. When the body was found, it was washed
and placed in the chariot which Harold used in the
fight. A large mound was raised and the chariot
was drawn into the mound by Harold's own horse.
The horse was now killed and Ring gave his own
saddle to Harold, telling him that he might ride or
drive to Valhalla just as it pleased him best. A
great memorial feast was held, and Ring bade his
warriors and nobles throw into the mound large

rings of gold and silver and good weapons before
it was finally closed.

The other account (in Saxo) tells how Ring
harnessed his own horse to Harold's chariot and
bade him drive quickly to Valhalla as the best in
battle, and when he came to Odin to prepare goodly
quarters for friend and foe alike. The pyre was then
kindled and by Ring's command the Danes placed
Harold's ship upon it. When the fire destroyed
the body, the king commanded his followers to walk
round the pyre and chant a lament, making rich
offerings of weapons, gold and treasure, so that the
fire might mount the higher in honour of the great
king. So the body was burned, the ashes were
collected, laid in an urn and sent to Leire, there to
be buried with the horse and the weapons in royal
fashion.

There are many curious coincidences of detail
between these accounts and that given by Ibn
Fadhlan of the burial of a Rûs warrior, and every
detail of them has at one time or another been
confirmed by archaeological evidence.

The dead were commemorated by the how itself,
but *bautasteinar*, i.e. memorial stones, were also
erected, either on the how or, more commonly,
elsewhere. In course of time these monuments came
to be inscribed with runes. Usually the inscription
is of the most formal type, giving the name of the

PLATE III

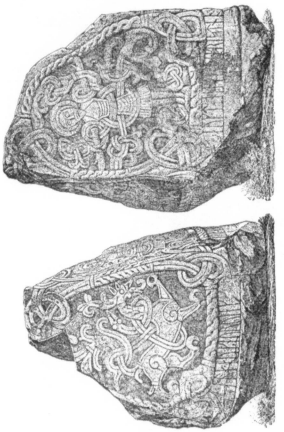

The Jellinge stone

dead person, the name of the man who raised the
memorial, and sometimes also that of the man who
carved the runes. Occasionally there is some more
human touch as in the wording of the Dyrna runes
(*v. supra*, p. 85), and in the latter part of the Viking
period we often find pictures and even scenes
inscribed on the stones. This is true of the Dyrna
stone (*v. supra*, p. 86): the Jellinge stone has a
figure of Christ on it, while there is a famous rock-
inscription in Sweden representing scenes from the
Sigurd-story (Regin's smithy, hammer, tongs and
bellows, Sigurd piercing Fafnir with his sword, the
birds whose speech Sigurd understood) encircled by
a serpent (Fafnir) bearing a long runic inscription.
The runic alphabet itself was the invention of an
earlier age. It is based chiefly on the old Roman
alphabet with such modifications of form and symbol
as were necessitated by the different sounds in the
Teutonic tongues and by the use of such unyielding
materials as wood and stone. Straight lines were
preferred to curved ones and sloping to horizontal.
During the Viking period it was simplified, and runic
inscriptions are found from the valley of the Dnieper
on the east to Man in the west, and from Iceland on
the north to the Piraeus in the south.

CHAPTER IX

SCANDINAVIAN INFLUENCE IN THE ORKNEYS, SHETLANDS, THE WESTERN ISLANDS AND MAN

OF all the countries visited by the Vikings it is undoubtedly the British Isles which bear most definitely the marks of their presence. The history and civilisation of Ireland, the Orkneys and Shetlands, the Western Islands and Man, Scotland and England, were profoundly affected by the Viking movement, and its influence is none the less interesting because it varies greatly from place to place, in both character and intensity. These variations are doubtless due in part to differences of political and social organisation as between Norsemen and Danes, or between men coming from scattered districts of the as yet loosely co-ordinated kingdoms of Denmark and Norway, but their chief cause lies in the wide divergences in the social and political conditions of the lands in which they settled.

The Orkneys and the Shetlands were settled by the Norsemen earlier than any other part of the British Isles and they formed part of the Norse kingdom till 1468. It is not surprising therefore that the great Norse historian Munch describes them as *ligesaa norskt som Norge selv,* 'as Norse as Norway itself.' The old Norse speech was still spoken there by a few people until the end of the 18th century, and we have a version of the ballad of *King Orfeo* taken down from recital at the close of that century with the Norse refrain still preserved '*Scowan ürla grün—Whar giorten han grün oarlac,*' i.e. probably *Skoven årle grön—Hvor hjorten han går årlig* = 'Early green's the wood—where the hart goes yearly.' Place-nomenclature is almost entirely Norse and the modern dialects are full of Norse words. Several runic inscriptions have been found, the most famous being that at Maeshowe in Hrossey, made by Norse crusaders when they wintered there in 1152–3 and amused themselves by breaking open the how, probably to look for treasure, and scoring their runes on the walls of the grave-chamber. In the system of landholding the 'udallers' are an interesting survival of the old Norse freeholders. 'The Udaller held his land without condition or limitation in any feudal sense,' says Mr Gilbert Goudie, i.e. he held his *udal* on precisely the same free terms that the native Norseman did his *óðal*. From the Shetlands and the Orkneys the Norsemen crossed to the Scottish mainland. Sutherland (i.e. the land south of the Orkneys), Caithness, Ross and Cromarty are full of Norse place-names, and Norse influence may be traced even further south.

M. 8

The Hebrides were also largely influenced by the Norsemen. Together with Man they formed a Norse kingdom down to the middle of the 13th century. Many of the islands themselves and their chief physical features bear Norse names, many personal names (e.g. MacAulay, son of Aulay or Olaf) are of Norse origin, and there are many Norse words in the Gaelic both of the islands and the mainland. These words have undergone extensive changes and much corruption in a language very different in form and sounds from that of their original source, and their recognition is a difficult problem. There is at present a danger of exaggerating this Norse element, the existence of which was long overlooked. Similarly, affinities have been traced between Scandinavian and Gaelic popular tales and folk-lore, but the evidence is too vague and uncertain to be of much value.

It is however in Man that we get the most interesting traces of the presence of the Norsemen. Here as elsewhere we have place-names and personal names bearing witness to their presence, but we have much else besides. Some 26 rune-inscribed crosses have been preserved to us. The crosses are Celtic in form and to a large extent in ornament also, but we find distinct traces of the Scandinavian animal-ornamentation. The inscriptions are short and for the most part give only the name of the memorial-raiser and the memorised. One bears the rune-writer's own proud boast 'Gaut made this and all in Man.' More interesting than the runes are the sculptured figures. On four of the crosses we have representations of incidents from the Sigurd story—Sigurd slaying Fafnir, Sigurd roasting Fafnir's heart and cooling his fingers in his mouth after trying too soon if the heart was done, Loki slaying the Otter. We also have pictures of Thor's adventure with the serpent of Miðgarðr and of Odin's last fight with Fenrir's Wolf. These sculptured stones are probably among the latest of those found in Man and have their chief parallel in stones found in Sweden (*v. supra*, p. 111). Possibly it was to settlers from Man also that we owe the famous Gosforth cross in Cumberland with its picture of Thor's fishing for the serpent.

In addition to all this we have the Manx legal system as a standing witness to Norse influence. The chief executive and legislative authority in the island (after the Governor) is the Tynwald Court. That court takes its name from the Old Norse *þing-völlr*[1], the plain where the *þing*[2] or popular assembly meets, and the House of Keys, which is the oldest division

[1] This word survives in another form in more than one Thing-wall among place-names.

[2] The word is familiar to us in the form *-ting* in *hus-ting*, house assembly (originally *hús-þing*), a council held by a king or earl and attended by his immediate followers, in contrast to the ordinary *þing* or general assembly of the people.

of the court, consisted originally of 24 members, a number perhaps due to Scandinavian influence, being a combination of two groups of 12 lawmen (*v. supra*, p. 103). These men who have the 'keys of the law' in their bosom closely resemble the 'lawmen' or speakers of the Icelandic assembly. All laws to be valid must be promulgated from the Tynwald Hill which corresponds to the *lögberg* or law-hill of the Icelandic *althing*. When the court is held the coroner 'fences' it against all disturbance or disorder, just as in the old Norwegian Gulathing we hear of *vé-bönd* or sanctuary-ropes drawn around the assembly.

It was possibly from Man that a good number of the Norse settlers in Cumberland, Westmorland and North Lancashire came (*v. infra*, pp. 126–7), and others may have settled in Galloway.

CHAPTER X

SCANDINAVIAN INFLUENCE IN IRELAND

At the time of the Viking invasion of Ireland the various provincial kingdoms were held in loose confederation under the authority of the *ardrí* or high king, but these kingdoms stood in constantly shifting relations of friendship and hostility towards one another, and were themselves often split into factions under rival chieftains. There was no national army like the English *fyrd*. Rather it consisted of a number of tribes, each commanded by its own chief, and though the chief owed allegiance to the king, the bond was a frail one. The tribe was further divided into *septs* and the army was utterly lacking in any cohesive principle. It is no wonder that for many years the Irish showed themselves quite unable to cope with the attacks of forces so well organised as those of the Norse and Danish Vikings.

In vivid contrast to the chaos in political and military organisation stand the missionary enthusiasm of the Irish church and the high level of education and culture which prevailed among her clergy and *literati*. In the Orkneys and the Shetlands such names as Papa Westray or Papa Stronsay bear witness to the presence of Irish priests or *papae* as the Norsemen called them. Irish anchorites had at one time settled in the Faroes (*v. supra*, p. 6), and when the Norsemen first settled in Iceland (c. 870) they found Irish monks already there. The monastic schools of Ireland were centres of learning and religious instruction for the whole of Western Europe, while Irish missionaries had founded monasteries in Italy, Switzerland, Germany and France.

Unfortunately religion and culture seem to have been almost entirely without influence on the body politic, and as the Vikings had at least in the early days no respect for the religion or the learning of the Irish nation there was nothing to prevent them from devastating Irish monasteries and carrying off the stores of treasured wealth which they contained. No plunder was more easily won, and it was only when they themselves had fallen under Christian influences and had come to appreciate Irish literary and artistic skill that they showed themselves more kindly disposed towards these homes of learning.

One feature must at once strike the observer who compares the Viking settlements in Ireland with those in England, viz. that Viking influence in Ireland is definitely concentrated in the great coast towns—Dublin, Wexford, Waterford, Cork and Limerick—and the districts immediately around them. Irish place-nomenclature bears very definite witness to this fact. *Ford-* in Strangford and Carlingford Loughs, Waterford and Wexford is O.N. *fjǫrðr*, a fjord, *-low* in Arklow and Wicklow is O.N. *ló*, 'low-lying, flat-grassland, lying by the water's edge.' The O.N. *ey*, an island, is found in Lambey, Dalkey, Dursey Head, Ireland's Eye (for Ireland's Ey), Howth is O.N. *höfuð*, 'a head,' Carnsore and Greenore Point contain O.N. *eyrr*, 'a sandy point pushing out into the sea.' Smerwick contains the familiar O.N. *vík* a bay or creek, while the Copeland Islands off Belfast lough are the O.N. *kaupmannaeyjar*, 'the merchants' islands.' All these are found on or off the coast, while the number of Scandinavian names found inland is extremely limited. The most interesting perhaps is Leixlip on the Liffey, a name derived from O.N. *laxahlaup*, 'salmon-leap.' Donegal, Fingall and Gaultiere are Celtic names, but they mark the presence of the northern *Gall* or foreigners, while the *-ster* in Ulster, Leinster and Munster is O.N. *-staðir* (pl. of *-staðr*, place, abode) suffixed to the old Gaelic names of these provinces.

There was free intermarriage between Norse and Irish (*v. supra*, p. 56), but the strength of the clan-system kept the races distinct and there was no such infiltration of the whole population as took place in the English Danelagh. This system prevented any such settlement of Norsemen upon their own farms as took place in England, and the invaders lived almost entirely in the coast towns and the districts in their immediate neighbourhood, busying themselves with trade and shipping.

Though the settlements were limited in their extent, we must not underrate their influence on Irish history generally. They gave the impetus there, as elsewhere, to the growth of town life, and from the period of Viking rule dates the origin of the

chief Irish towns. To them also was due the great
expansion, if not the birth, of Irish trade. Mention
has been made of the wealth of Limerick (*v. supra*,
p. 97), drawn chiefly from trade with France and
Spain, and the other towns were not behind
Limerick. The naval power of Dublin stretched from
Waterford to Dundalk, the Irish channel swarmed
with Viking fleets, and many of the shipping terms in
use in Gaelic are loan-words from the Norse.

It is probably to the trading activities of Vikings
from the chiefs ports of Ireland that we owe the
sprinkling of names of Norse origin which we find
along the Welsh coast from the Dee to the Severn—
Great Orm's Head, Anglesey, Ramsey I, Skokholm
Island, Flat Holme and Steep Holme, and to them
may be due the establishment of Swansea, earlier
Sweinesea, Haverfordwest and possibly Bideford, as
Norse colonies in the Bristol channel. We know in
later times of several Norsemen who were living in
Cardiff, Bristol, Swansea and Haverfordwest.

Norse influence in Ireland probably reached its
climax in the 10th century. The battle of Clontarf
offered a serious check and though there was still a
succession of Norse kings and earls in Dublin they
had to acknowledge the authority of the *ardrí*. The
line of Sigtryggr of the Silken Beard came to an end
by the middle of the 11th century, and the rulership
of Dublin fell into the hands of various Norse families

from other Irish settlements and from Man and the Isles. From 1078-94 it was under the rule of the great conqueror Godred Crovan from Man, and its connexion with that kingdom was only severed finally when Magnus Barefoot came on his great Western expedition in 1103, and brought Man into direct allegiance to the kings of Norway. Celtic influence must have been strong in the Norse families themselves. Several of the kings bear Gaelic names, and it is probably from this period that such familiar names as MacLamont or MacCalmont, MacIver, and MacQuistan date, where the Gaelic patronymic prefix has been added to the Norse names Lagmaðr, Ívarr and Eysteinn. While Norse power in Dublin was on the decline as a political force it is curious to note that the vigorous town-life and the active commerce instituted by the Norse settlers made that city of ever-increasing importance as a centre of Irish life and Irish interests generally, and there can be no question that it was the Norsemen who really made Dublin the capital city of Ireland.

The Norse element remained absolutely distinct, not only in Dublin but also in the other cities in which they had settled, right down to the time of the English invasion in the 12th century. Frequent mention is made of them in the records of the great towns, and they often both claimed and received privileges quite different from those accorded to the native Irish or to the English settlers. They were known to the latter as 'Ostmen' or 'Easterlings,' a term which in this connexion seems to have ousted the earlier *Norvagienses* or *les Norreys, les Norwicheis*. The term 'Ostman' doubtless represents O.N. *Austmaðr*, a man dwelling to the east. Exactly how or where it first came to be applied to Norsemen it is difficult to say. The word has left its mark in Oxmanstown, earlier Ostmanstown, the district of the city of Dublin assigned to the Ostmen by the English invaders.

Learning and religion in Ireland suffered grievously from Norse attack but not so sorely as in England. There was never a time when so dark a picture could have been drawn of Irish learning as Alfred gives of the state of English learning when he translated the *Pastoral Care*, and when once the Vikings began to form settlements they were themselves strongly affected by the wealth of literary and artistic skill with which they found themselves brought into contact. The question of Irish influence on Norse mythology and literature is a much vexed one. At present we are suffering from a reaction against exaggerated claims made on its behalf some thirty years ago, but while refusing to accept the view that Norse legends, divine and heroic alike, are based on a wholesale refashioning and recreating of stories from Celtic saga-lore, it would be idle to deny that

the contact between the two nations must have been
fertile of result and that Norse literature in form,
style and subject-matter alike, bears many marks of
Gaelic influence.

CHAPTER XI

SCANDINAVIAN INFLUENCE IN ENGLAND

OF the districts occupied by Scandinavian settlers
in England the ones which show their presence most
strongly are Cumberland, Westmorland, North Lancashire and Yorkshire in the old kingdom of Northumbria and the district of the Five Boroughs in the
midlands.   East Anglia was not so deeply affected
by the Danish occupation.

Before dealing with one of the chief sources of
our knowledge of the presence of Norse and Danish
settlers in various parts of England, viz. the evidence
derived from place-nomenclature, a few words must
be said as to the chief Scandinavian elements which
can be recognised in English place-names.

Of elements other than personal names the
commonest are as follows, several of them being
used as independent words to this day in English
dialects which have been affected by Scandinavian
influence :—

-BECK.   O.N. *bekkr*, brook, small stream of
water.

-BIGGIN(G). O.N. *bygging*, building.

-BY. O.N. *bør*, Dan. Swed. *by*, town or village. This word indicates a Danish rather than a Norse settlement.

-CAR(R), -ker. O.N. *kjarr*, *kjörr*, brushwood, especially on swampy ground.

-DALE. O.N. *dalr*, valley. Etymologically this word might be of native English origin but its distribution points to Norse influence.

-FELL. O.N. *fjall*, mountain.

-FORCE. O.N. *fors*, waterfall.

-FORTH. O.N. *fjǫrðr*, fjord. English -ford and Scandinavian -forth often interchange in the old documents.

-GARTH. O.N. *garðr*, enclosure, the Scandinavian equivalent of English 'yard.'

-GILL. O.N. *gil*, deep narrow glen with a stream at the bottom.

-HOLM. O.N. *holmr*, small island especially in a bay, creek, or river. In England its meaning was further developed and it often means 'low-lying level ground on the borders of a river or stream.' Now often concealed in the suffix -ham.

-KELD. O.N. *kelda*, well, spring.

-LUND, -lound. O.N. *lundr*, grove. Now often corrupted to -land in English place-names.

-MIRE. O.N. *myrr*, moor, bog, swamp.

-RAISE. O.N. *hreysi*, cairn.

-SCALE. O.N. *skali*, house. This word is Norse rather than Danish.

-SCAR, -skear, -skerry. O.N. *sker*, isolated rock in the sea.

-SCOUT. O.N. *skúti*, cave formed by jutting rocks.

-SCOUGH, -scow. O.N. *skógr*, wood.

-SLACK. O.N. *slakki*, slope on a mountain edge. Often used in English place-names of a hollow or boggy place[1].

-TARN. O.N. *tjörn*, small lake.

-THORP(E). O.N. *þorp*, hamlet, village. This word is also found in O.E. and in some place-names is undoubtedly of native origin, but its general distribution points fairly conclusively to Norse influence.

-THWAITE. O.N. *þveit*, parcel of land, paddock.

-TOFT. O.N. *topt*, piece of ground, messuage, homestead.

-WITH. O.N. *viðr*, a wood.

-WATH. O.N. *vað*, a ford.

Place-names with the prefix *Norman-* mark the settlement not of Normans but of Norsemen (or Northmen as the English called them), as in Normanton and Normanby, while the settlement of Danes is marked by the prefix *Dena-* or *Den-* as in Denaby and Denby. This latter prefix however has other sources as well.

---

[1] In Scotland it is used of a hollow pass in a ridge.

Scandinavian personal names are very common in place-names but their presence can as a rule only be detected with any degree of certainty by reference to the forms found in early documents. Among the more easily recognised are *Grímr*, as in Grimsargh (Lancs.) and Grimsby (Lincs.), *Gunnarr*, as in Gunnerside (Yorks.), *Ketill*, as in Kettlewell (Yorks.), *Klakkr*, as in Claxton (Norf.), *Ormr*, as in Ormskirk (Lancs.). Others, to be found by reference to earlier forms, are *Fráni*, as in Franesfeld (= Farnsfield, Notts.), *Gamall*, as in Gamelestune (= Gamston, Notts.), *Gunnúlfr*, as in Gunnulveston (= Gonalston, Notts.), *Knútr*, as in Cnutestone (= Knuston, Northants.), *Leifr*, as in Levesbi (= Laceby, Lincs.), *Sumarliði*, as in Sumarlidebi (= Somerby, Lincs.), *Skúli*, as in Sculetuna (= Scoulton, Norf.), *Tóli*, as in Toleslund (= Toseland, Hunts.), *Víkingr*, as in Wichingestone (= Wigston, Leic.), *Úlfr*, as in Ulvesbi (= Ulceby, Lincs.).

Examining the distribution of Scandinavian place-names determined by the above tests and others which can be applied with great accuracy, if we study not the modern but the old forms of the place-names, we find that the place-nomenclature of Cumberland and Westmorland is almost entirely either Scandinavian or Celtic. Indeed it would seem that the Anglian settlement had hardly affected these districts at all, and it was reserved for the

Scandinavian settlers to Teutonise them. The same is true of Furness and Lancashire, north of the Ribble, whose old names Stercaland and Agmundernesse are of Norse origin, but south of that river there is a great diminution of Norse place-names except along the coast and a little way inland, where we have several -*bys* and -*dales*. In Cheshire the evidence of Scandinavian settlement is confined almost entirely to the Wirral, but there the large number of -*bys* and place-names like Thingwall (*v. supra*, p. 115, note 1) point to a strong Viking colony, and the distribution of place-names in South Lancashire and Cheshire bears witness to active intercourse between the settlers in Ireland and England.

On the other side of the Pennine chain, though Northumberland was several times ravaged by the Norsemen and was probably well populated at least in the fertile river-valleys, there is practically no evidence of their presence to be found in place-names. There are several Biggins, Carrs, and Holms, a few Tofts and Dales, but these are common dialect words and usually found in uncompounded forms. They are practically never found in names of towns or villages, and may well have been introduced from districts further south. In the extreme west and south-west of the county there are 'fells' and 'dales' but these are on the borders of Cumberland, Westmorland and Durham. The small streams are 'burns' and not 'becks,' the Wansbeck being a corruption of an earlier *Wanespike.*

When we cross into co. Durham the tributaries of the Wear vary between 'burn' and 'beck,' but by the time we reach the Tees these have all become becks. Beechburn Beck, a tributary of the Wear, shows how a Scandinavian term could be attached to an English name, when its own meaning was neglected or forgotten. Other Scandinavian names are common, but as in Northumberland they belong to the dialect generally and are seldom found in names of towns or villages. Viking settlers must have been few in numbers and widely scattered throughout these two counties. One great exception must be named among the towns, viz. Durham itself. The city was named *Dún-holmr,* 'the hill-island,' by the Vikings, and its present name is only the Norman corruption of that form.

South of the Tees we find ourselves in a district whose place-names are to a very large extent Scandinavian, and Norse settlements are thickly and evenly distributed from the North Sea to the Pennine chain.

Passing from Northumbria to the Danelagh, Lincolnshire is perhaps more purely Scandinavian in its place-names than any other English county. In Derbyshire Viking influence is not so strong but the county was probably very thinly inhabited at least

in the north and west and did not offer attractive
settling ground.   Derby itself was rechristened by
the Northmen, its earlier name being 'Norðweorðig.'
The rich fields and pastures of Leicestershire attracted
a great many settlers and Nottinghamshire is also
strongly Scandinavian.   Rutland and Northamptonshire are strongly Danish except that there is some
shading off towards the S.W. corner of the latter
county.   In the country bordering the Danelagh on
the south and west, Staffordshire has a few Scandinavian place-names on its Derbyshire and Leicestershire borders, while Warwickshire has several on its
Leicestershire and Northamptonshire borders.

In East Anglia Danish settlements must have
been numerous in the north and east especially
towards the coast, but their presence is less strongly
marked in the S.W. portion of the county.   In
Suffolk they are confined still more definitely to the
coast-districts and the Danes do not seem to have
settled in the south of the county at all.   Three
Kirbys near the Essex coast mark settlements in that
county.   Of the other border-counties Huntingdonshire, Cambridgeshire and Bedfordshire show only
the slightest traces of Scandinavian influence in their
place-nomenclature, though we know from other
evidence that there must have been many Danish
settlers in these counties.

Closely allied to the evidence of place-names is

M.   9

that of dialect. A very large number of words
definitely of Scandinavian origin are found in the
dialects of N.E. and N.W. England, in the N. Midlands
and East Anglia, but they do not furnish so sensitive
a test as do place-names for the extent of the
Scandinavian settlements and they need not be dis-
cussed here.

More interesting as evidence of the deep influence
of the Viking settlers on our language is the large
number of Scandinavian loan-words which have
become part of our standard speech, many of them
being words essential to our every-day talk. To
Scandinavian influence we owe the pronouns *they*,
them and *their*, the adjectives *same* and *both*, the *fro*
in *to* and *fro* and possibly the auxiliary *are* and
the preposition *till*. These last are found in the
Northumbrian dialect of Old English but their
widespread use is probably due to Scandinavian
influence. In addition to these we may note the
following :

Verbs : *bait, bask, batten, call, cast, dawn, droop,
drown, gain, gabble, ransack, scare, scour, scrape,
skim, skip, squeal, stint, take,*

Nouns : *anger, billow, boon, dusk, fellow, gait,
grime, haven, husband, husk, husting, scull, scurf,
skill, skin, skirt, sky, window,*

Adjectives : *awkward, ill, odd, rotten, scant, sly,
ugly, weak,*

and a good many words in which Scandinavian forms
have replaced the cognate English ones, e.g. *aloft,
athwart, awe, birth, egg, get, gift, give, guest, raid,
sister, swain, Thursday.*

These words are for the most part of the very
stuff and substance of our language, giving vivid
expression to clear-cut ideas, and though numeri-
cally they are outnumbered by the loan-words from
French, they are in themselves more essential to our
speech than the rich vocabulary derived from that
language.

For the extent and character of the Viking
settlements in England we have however a far more
delicate and accurate index than that to be found in
the evidence of place-names and dialects. When we
study the pages of Domesday, the great record of
English social organisation in the 11th century, we
find that in the counties which came under Viking
influence there are many details of land-division,
tenure, assessment and social organisation generally
wherein those counties differ from the rest of England,
and some of these differences can still be traced.

The 'ridings' of Yorkshire and the Lindsey division
of Lincolnshire were originally 'thrithings' (O.N.
þriþjungr, a third part), the initial *th* being later
absorbed by the final consonant of the preceding
'East,' 'West,' 'North' and 'South' (in Lincs.).

The chief tests of Scandinavian influence, drawn

from Domesday and allied sources, are however as follows :

(1) The use of the Danish 'wapentake' as the chief division of the county in contrast to the English 'hundred.' This is found in Lincolnshire, Derbyshire (with one exception on its southern border), Nottinghamshire, Leicestershire, Rutland, and one district of Northamptonshire, now included in Rutland. We have wapentakes in Yorkshire, except in certain districts along the sea-coast, while in Lancashire the term was applied to the court of the hundred or shire long after the Conquest. There is some evidence also for the belief that the use of the hundred (or wapentake) as an administrative unit is in itself due to Scandinavian influence. The proportion of names of hundreds (or wapentakes) which are definitely of Danish origin is very high and, unless we assume wholesale renaming, this points to their having been first named at a period subsequent to the Danish conquest.

(2) The assessment by carucates in multiples and submultiples of 12 is characteristic of the Danelagh, as opposed to that by hides, arranged on a decimal system in the strictly English districts. This is found in Derbyshire, Nottinghamshire, Lincolnshire, Leicestershire and Rutland, with the exception of the above mentioned district. There are traces of a duodecimal assessment in the two N.E. hundreds of

Northamptonshire, while in Lancashire a hidal assessment has been superimposed upon an original carucal
one. Carucal assessment is found also in Yorkshire,
Norfolk and Suffolk.

(3) In Lincolnshire, Nottinghamshire, Derbyshire
and Yorkshire we have traces of the use of the Danish
'long' hundred (= 120), e.g. the fine for breaking the
king's peace is £8, i.e. 120 ores[1] of 16 pence.

Using the various tests we find that the Scandinavian kingdom of Northumbria was considerably
smaller than the earlier realm of that name, Northumberland and Durham being but sparsely settled,
while South Lancashire and Cheshire were occupied
chiefly along the coast. The kingdom would seem to
fall into two isolated halves, Cumberland and Westmorland and North Lancashire in the north-west
and Yorkshire in the south-east. The district of the
Five Boroughs covered Derbyshire, Nottinghamshire,
Lincolnshire (Lincoln and Stamford), Leicestershire,
and probably the whole of Rutland (Stamford). The
case of Northamptonshire is difficult. The carucal
assessment fails except in the extreme N.E. of the
county, but Danish place-nomenclature is strongly
evident, though it shades off somewhat towards the
S.W. It resembles Danish East Anglia rather than

---

[1] The *ore* as a unit of weight for silver is of Scandinavian origin.
In some districts it was of the value of 16 pence, in others of 20 pence,
and eight *ores* went to the *mark*.

the district of the Five Boroughs and it is possible
that the boundary of Guthrum's East Anglian kingdom,
which is only carried as far as Stony Stratford in
the peace of Alfred and Guthrum, really ran along
Watling Street for a few miles, giving two-thirds of
that county to the East Anglian realm.

Northumbria was governed by a succession of
kings. The Five Boroughs formed a loose confederation, and there can be no question that the districts
which 'obeyed' (*v. supra*, p. 31) the boroughs of Derby,
Leicester, Nottingham, Lincoln (and Stamford) and
Northampton form the modern counties named from
these towns. It is also to Danish influence direct or
indirect that we owe the similar organisation of the
counties of Huntingdonshire, Cambridgeshire, Bedfordshire and Hertfordshire in the old East Anglian
kingdom. Each of these counties had a *jarl* or earl,
whose headquarters were at the 'borough.' He sum-
moned the *here*, whether for political or military
purposes, and when these counties passed once more
under English rule he fulfilled the functions of the
older *ealdorman*.

In East Anglia, apart from place-names (*v. supra*,
p. 129) and carucal assessment in Norfolk and Suffolk,
we are left with the boundaries of Guthrum's kingdom
and with various miscellaneous evidence for estimating
the extent of Scandinavian influence. There is a
curious 'hundredus Dacorum' (cf. *supra*, p. 10) in

Hertfordshire, while the *Historia Eliensis* and other documents tend to show the presence of a strong Danish element in the population and social organisation of the districts around Cambridge. The kingship of East Anglia came to an end early in the 10th century, and it is probable that its organisation was then changed to one resembling that of the Five Boroughs, viz. a number of districts grouped around central 'boroughs,' which afterwards became counties, except in the older divisions of Norfolk and Suffolk.

A careful study of Domesday and other authorities reveals many other features of interest in our social system which were due to Viking influence. Certain types of manorial structure are specially common in the Danelagh. Manor and vill are by no means identical, indeed several manors are included under one vill. Very frequent is the type which consists in a central manor with sokeland appurtenant. In the Danelagh there was a large number of small freeholders and the free peasant class was much more numerous than in Anglo-Saxon England. These districts stand in clear contrast to the strongly manorialised southern counties and they were not feudalised to any appreciable extent before the Norman conquest. When that system was imposed we often find single knight's fees having to be taken over by entire communities of sokemen. The 'holds' of Northumbria, who rank next after the earls,

and the 'drengs' of Cumberland, Westmorland,
Lancashire, Northumberland and Durham, are also
of Scandinavian origin. The 'dreng' was 'a free
servant of the king endowed with lands' and the
name still survives in the Yorkshire place-name
Dringhouses.

The legal instinct was strong in the Scandinavian
mind and English law bears deep marks of its influence.
The very word 'law' itself is of Scandinavian origin
and has replaced the English 'doom.' The chief
judicial authority in Lincoln, Stamford, Cambridge,
Chester and York was in the hands of twelve
lagmen or *judices*. These 'lawmen' (*v. supra*, p. 103)
though they had judicial authority were not chosen
by the king or by popular election. Their position
was hereditary. Of special interest are the '12 senior
thanes' of Aethelred's laws for the Five Boroughs
enacted at Wantage in 997. They have to come
forward in the court of every wapentake and to
swear that they will not accuse wrongly any innocent
man or conceal any guilty one. The exact force of
this enactment has been a matter of dispute—whether
the thanes simply bore witness to the personal status
of the accused, thus enabling the court to determine
the ordeal through which he should be put, or whether
we have an anticipation of the system of presentment
by jury. Whatever may be the exact truth there
can be little doubt, says Dr Vinogradoff, that

such a custom prepared the way for the indictment jury of the 12th century. The same author attributes to Danish influence a new conception of crime. It is no longer merely a breach of the peace or the result of a feud, to be settled by monetary compensation, it is a breach of that conception of honour which binds together military societies. The criminal is now branded as *nithing*, a man unworthy of comradeship with his fellow-warriors.

Unfortunately it is only within the last few years that the question of Danish influence on our social, political and legal systems has been treated at all seriously and much work still remains to be done, but we can already see that the Danes affected English life far more deeply than a superficial glance might suggest. Doubtless the Danish invasions struck a heavy blow at learning and literature, a blow from the effects of which not even the heroic activities of an Alfred could save them, but there can be no question that in the development of town life, in the promotion of trade, in the improvement of organisation and administration, in the modification of legal procedure the invaders conferred great benefits on the country as a whole.

CHAPTER XII

SCANDINAVIAN INFLUENCE IN THE EMPIRE
AND ICELAND

CONSIDERING the long and devastating campaign of the Vikings within the Frankish empire and more especially within its western portion, it is surprising that they only formed permanent settlements in one small area, leaving practically no marks of their presence elsewhere. Great portions of the Low Countries were in almost continuous occupation by them during the 9th century, but the opportunity was lost, and beyond an important share in the development of the trade of Duurstede, the Vikings hardly left a sign of their influence behind them.

The case of Normandy is different. Here we have a definite district assigned to the invaders, just as the Danelagh was given to them in England, and the whole of that territory is deeply impregnated with their influence. Many of the Norman towns in *-ville* contain as the first element in their name a Norse personal name, e.g. Catteville, Cauverville, Colleville, Fouqueville, Hacqueville containing the names *Káte, Kálfr, Kolr, Fólki, Hákon*, while the suffixes *-bec, -beuf, -dale, -ey, -gard, -londe, -torp, -tot, -tuit,*

-*vic* as in Bolbec, Elbeuf, Saussedalle, Jersey, Eppe-
gard, Mandelonde, Torgistorp, Abbetot, Bracquetuit,
Barvic go back to O.N. *bekkr, búð* (booth), *dalr, ey*
(island), *garðr, lundr, þorp, topt, þveit, vík* (*v. supra,*
pp. 124—5). The dialect of Normandy to this day
contains a good number of Scandinavian words,
and others have been introduced into the standard
language. Some of these have also found their way
into English through our Norman conquerors, e.g.
*abet, baggage, elope, equip, jolly, rubbish, scoop,
strife* just as the *Bulbeck* in Swaffham Bulbeck
(Cambs.) and Bulbeck Common above Blanchland in
Northumberland is from the great Norman barony
of Bulbeck, so named after Bolbec in Normandy, of
which they once formed part. Norman law and
customs also show many traces of Scandinavian
influence and so does Norman folk-lore.

The Normans still looked to Denmark as their
home-land down to the end of the 10th century, and at
least twice during the reign of Harold Blue-tooth their
Dukes received help from that country. The nobles
soon ceased to speak their old northern language, but
it is probable that it remained current on the lips of
the people for some considerable time longer.

The Vikings always showed themselves keenly
sensitive to the influence of a civilisation higher or
more developed than their own, and this is nowhere
more apparent than in Normandy. Heathenism

found a champion as late as 943 when, on the death
of William Longsword, a rising of heathen Normans
was crushed with the aid of the Frankish king, but
for the most part the Normans soon showed themselves devout sons of the Church and were destined
in the 11th century to be numbered among the
most ardent supporters of the Crusades. With the
adoption of Christianity they learned to respect and
honour those homes of learning which they had once
devastated for their wealth of hoarded treasure, and
the famous school at Bec, whence came Lanfranc and
Anselm, was only one among many which they richly
endowed and supported.

Their religious and artistic feeling found expression in that development of Romanesque architecture which we know as Norman and which has
given so many famous buildings not only to Normandy
but to England, to Sicily and to Southern Italy
generally. In literature the Norman-French *trouvères*
did much towards popularising the romances of war
and adventure which play so important a part in
medieval literature, and when they settled in England
it was largely due to Anglo-Norman poets that 'the
matter of Britain' became one of the great subjects
of romance for all time.

In its social organisation Normandy seems speedily
to have been feudalised. Rollo divided the land
among a comparatively small number of large

landholders and the system of land tenure was quite different from that in the English Danelagh with its large number of small freeholders. On the other hand it was probably due to Norse traditions of personal freedom that serfdom disappeared earlier in Normandy than in any other of the French provinces.

Trade and commerce were fostered here as everywhere by the Vikings. It was the Normans who first taught the French to become a power at sea, many French naval terms are of Norman origin and from the Norman province have come some of France's greatest sea-captains.

The Vikings like the Franks before them threw off their old speech and submitted to the all-embracing power of Latin civilisation, and the result was a race endowed with vigorous personality, untiring activity, and the instinct for ruling men. The Normans may have become largely French but they lost none of their old enterprise and spirit of adventure. In the 11th century they conquered England and founded great kingdoms for themselves in Sicily and South Italy. No Viking stock was more vigorous than that which resulted from the grafting of Gallo-Latin culture on the ruder civilisation of the Teutonic north.

Their influence on France as a whole is not nearly as great as the influence of their kinsmen in England, probably because English government was centralised

(under Norman rule) much sooner than French
government, and their influence was thus able to
make itself felt outside the actual districts in which
they settled. The settlement of Normandy helped
however towards the consolidation of power in the
hands of Charles the Bald and his successors, much
as the settlement of the Danelagh helped in establishing the final supremacy of Wessex.

It remains to speak of one great home of Viking
civilisation to which more than one reference has
been made in previous chapters, viz. Iceland. The
story of its settlement is a very simple one. It
commenced about 870, when many great Norwegian
noblemen sought there for themselves and their
followers a freer life than they could obtain under
the growing power of Harold Fairhair. It was
greatly strengthened by settlers both from Norway
and from Ireland and the Western Islands when that
power was firmly established by the battle of Hafrsfjord, and by the year 930 the settlement was
practically complete. Iceland was more purely
Scandinavian than any other settlement made during
the Viking age. Here we have not the case of one
civilisation grafted on another and earlier one as in
England, Ireland or the Frankish empire, but the
transference of the best and finest elements in a
nation to new and virgin soil where, for good or ill,
they were free to develop their civilisation on almost

entirely independent lines. Settlers from the Western
Islands and from Ireland may have brought Celtic
elements, and Christianity was not without influence,
when it was introduced from Norway at the close of
the 10th century, but on the whole we see in Iceland
just what Viking civilisation was capable of when
left to itself.

At first the settlers lived in almost complete
isolation, political and religious, from one another,
but they soon found that some form of organisation
was necessary and groups of settlers began by choosing from among their number a *goði*, or chieftain,
half-priest, half-leader, who was the speaker at their
moot and their representative in negotiation with
neighbouring groups. Then, continued disputes and
the lack of a common law led to the establishment
of a central moot or *alþing*, with a speaker to
speak one single law for all. But the Norsemen
were much better at making constitutions and
enacting laws than they were at observing them
when instituted, and the condition of Iceland has
been vividly if roughly summarised as one of 'all
law and no government.' The local *þings* or the
national *alþing* might enact perfect laws, but there
was no compelling force, except public opinion, to
make them be obeyed. Even the introduction of
Christianity made no difference : the Icelanders
quarrelled as bitterly over questions of ecclesiastical

as of civil law and the authorities of the medieval
Church were scandalised by their anarchic love of
freedom. In the words of Professor Ker 'the settlers
made a commonwealth of their own, which was in
contradiction to all the prejudices of the middle ages
and of all ancient and modern political philosophy ;
a commonwealth which was not a state, which had
no government, no sovereignty.' 'It was anarchy
without a police-constable.' The result was that the
rich men grew richer, the poor became poorer, the
smaller gentry died out and the large estates fell
into fewer and fewer hands. The great men quarrelled
among themselves, intrigued against one another and
played into the hands of the Norwegian kings who
were only waiting their opportunity. It came in the
days of Hákon the Old. 'Land and thanes' were
sworn into subjection to that king at the Althing in
1262, and in 1271 the old Icelandic common law was
superseded by a new Norse code.

The failure of the Icelandic commonwealth is
amply compensated for by the rich intellectual development of Icelandic literature, which owed many
of its most characteristic features to the fact that it
was written in a land almost completely isolated
and detached from the main currents of Western
medieval thought and the general trend of European
history, but in itself that failure is full of deepest
import for a right understanding of the part played

by Viking civilisation in Europe. Powerful and highly developed as that civilisation was in many ways, it only reached its highest and best expression when brought into fruitful contact with other and older civilisations. There it found the corrective for certain inherent weaknesses, more especially for certain tendencies of too strongly individualistic character leading to political and intellectual anarchy, while at the same time by its own energy and vigour it quickened the life of the older civilisations where they were tending to become effete or outworn. The Germanic peoples had done much for the development of European civilisation in the time of the wanderings of the nations, but by the end of the 8th century they had lost much of their pristine vigour through contact with the richer and more luxurious civilisation of the Roman world. It was reserved for the North Germanic peoples, or the Northmen as we can more fitly describe them, in the 9th and 10th centuries to give a yet more powerful stimulus to European life, if not to European thought, a stimulus which perhaps found its highest expression in the great creations of the Norman race in the world of politics, the world of commerce, the world of architecture and the world of letters.

BIBLIOGRAPHY

[The appended bibliography does not attempt to deal with primary authorities, with the large mass of valuable periodical literature which has been published within the last thirty years, or with books only incidentally concerned with the movement. It is much to be regretted that so few of the important Scandinavian books on the subject have been translated into English.]

BJÖRKMAN, E. Scandinavian Loan-words in Middle English. Halle. 1906.

BUGGE, A. Vikingerne. 2 series. Christiania. 1904–6. (German trans. of 1st series. Leipzig. 1896.)

—— Vesterlandenes Inflydelse paa Nordboernes i Vikingetiden. Christiania. 1905.

—— Norges Historie. Vol. I, Pt. II. Christiania. 1910.

COLLINGWOOD, W. G. Scandinavian Britain. London. 1908.

CRAIGIE, W. A. The Religion of Ancient Scandinavia. London. 1906.

DIETRICHSON, L. and MEYER, S. Monumenta Orcadica. Christiania. 1906. (Abridged English edition.)

DU CHAILLU, P. B. The Viking Age. 2 vols. London. 1889.

GUSTAFSON, G. Norges Oldtid. Christiania. 1906.

HENDERSON, G. The Norse Influence on Celtic Scotland. Glasgow. 1910.

KEARY, C. F. The Vikings in Western Christendom. London. 1891.

KERMODE, P. M. C. Manx Crosses. London. 1907.

MAURER, K. Die Bekehrung des Norwegischen Stammes. 2 vols. Munich. 1855-9.

MONTELIUS, O. Sveriges Historia. Vol. I. Stockholm. 1903. (German tr. Kulturgeschichte Schwedens. Leipzig. 1906.)

MÜLLER, S. Vor Oldtid. Copenhagen. 1897. (German tr. Nordische Altertümskunde. 2 vols. Strasburg. 1897-8.)

OLRIK, A. Nordisk Aaandsliv i Vikingetid. Copenhagen. 1907. (German tr. Nordisches Geistesleben. Heidelberg. 1908.)

STEENSTRUP, J. C. H. R. Normannerne. 4 vols. Copenhagen. 1876-82.

—— Danmarks Riges Historie. Vol. I. Copenhagen. 1876-82.

THOMSEN, V. The Relations between Ancient Russia and Scandinavia. Oxford. 1877.

VOGEL, W. Die Normannen und das Fränkische Reich. Heidelberg. 1906.

VOGT, L. J. Dublin som Norsk By. Christiania. 1906.

The Publications of the Viking Club (Saga-Book and Year Book) include papers on various aspects of the movement and notices of the literature of the subject as well as descriptions of various archaeological discoveries.

INDEX

Lightning Source UK Ltd.
Milton Keynes UK
UKOW052312070312

188553UK00001B/15/P

9 781107 606005